T0345267

GRASSES

Reaktion's Botanical series is the first of its kind, integrating horticultural and botanical writing with a broader account of the cultural and social impact of trees, plants and flowers.

Published

Bamboo Susanne Lucas
Geranium Kasia Boddy
Grasses Stephen A. Harris
Lily Marcia Reiss
Oak Peter Young
Pine Laura Mason
Willow Alison Syme
Yew Fred Hageneder

GRASSES

☙❧

Stephen A. Harris

REAKTION BOOKS

Published by
REAKTION BOOKS LTD
33 Great Sutton Street
London EC1V 0DX, UK

www.reaktionbooks.co.uk

First published 2014
Copyright © Stephen A. Harris 2014

Printed and bound in China by Toppan Printing Co., Ltd

A catalogue record for this book is available from the British Library

ISBN 978 1 78023 273 7

Contents

ଓଔ

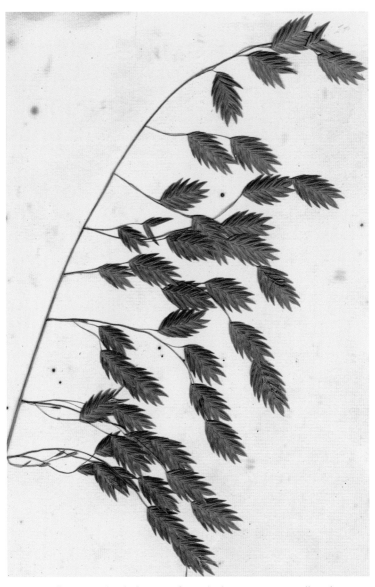

Inflorescence detail of sea oats, from a herbarium specimen collected by the English explorer Mark Catesby in South Carolina in 1723.

one

Dominating the Planet
࿔࿔

That grasses are interesting and important plants is a fact recog-
nised by botanists all the world over, yet it would appear that
people in general can hardly have appreciated either their interest
or their importance.

HARRY MARSHALL WARD, *Grasses* (1901)

The word 'grass', with its origin in Old English, is cognate to two
other words so characteristic of these plants: 'green' and 'grow'.
Our cultures are full of references to grasses and the products
made from them. Grass is the first plant mentioned in the Genesis
creation myth according to the King James Bible. We talk of grass
being greener on the other side of the fence, not letting grass grow
under our feet, the green grass of home, that all flesh is grass, being
put out to grass and kicking things into the long grass. 'Bread' is syn-
onymous with food or a slang term for money. Beer and whisky, also
products of grasses, provide regular pleasure for millions of people.
Edward Elgar's music conjures images of rolling, grass-covered hills
in English landscapes. Village greens and thatched cottages add to
such romantic chocolate-box rural clichés. Acres of manicured lawns,
playing fields and sports arenas cultivate conflicting impressions of
learning, peace, fair play and multimillion-pound businesses. Thousands
of square kilometres of rolling South African veld and North American
prairie, under vast skies, are associated with ambiguous cultural icons
such as the *voortrekker* and cowboy. 'Keep off the grass' is a familiar

7

refrain of petty authority, and when translated into Portuguese (*não pise na grama*) is a source of mild amusement to English speakers. Grass transforms landscapes, erases people's memories and renders the corrupt clean. Grasses even heralded the age of perpetual light when, in 1854, the German watchmaker Heinrich Göbel used a carbonized bamboo filament to produce the first light bulb. Our relationships with grasses are profound, and have been for tens of thousands of years. Yet we are not the only organisms to have such intimate relationships; thousands of other plants, animals and fungi need grasses and the habitats they create. The giant panda, munching on bamboo, is an iconic image of the global conservation movement and symbolic of the dependence of animals on grass.

Humans have taken this group of plants and become dependent upon it. By 2030 we will need twice the amount of food we produce today, while twenty years after that the human population is expected to reach more than nine billion. Furthermore, 90 per cent of the planet's land area will have been affected by human activities, and mean global surface temperature will have risen by up to 6°C. If we are to feed ourselves we must either continue to adapt grasses to our life-styles, or our behaviours must adapt to the needs of grasses. Land used for growing grass as food, and perhaps fuel, must also be balanced against where we wish to live and stewardship of the places where the planet's wild grasses grow.

This book uses familiar grasses to explore interactions between grass biology and humans since the end of the last ice age. The first three chapters introduce the essentials of grass biology, including the plants that are often confused with grasses. Chapters on wheat, maize, rice and sugar follow, and focus on grasses as catalysts for civilization, crop domestication, food production in the face of population growth and the ways in which human societies have changed in response to the use of grasses. Relationships among grasses and fungi, both positive and negative, are the subject of the next chapter. This is followed by chapters on the use of grasses as forage, fuel and recreational spaces, and finally by a chapter on the role of grasses as weeds. The present chapter introduces grass morphology and naming, before exploring the evolutionary relationships of the grass family and its origin.

Grasses as Plants

As plants, grasses are essential for converting the energy of sunlight into sugars; they are the fuel of life on Earth. Grasses (Poaceae, or Gramineae, family) are essential parts of global ecosystems, and are by far the most important plant family for humans. Four species (wheat, rice, maize and sugar) provide 60 per cent of people's calorie intake either directly, or indirectly as livestock food. The Poaceae is the fifth most speciose plant family; more than 11,000 grass species are known.

Antarctic hairgrass, one of only two Antarctic flowering plants, grows rapidly in the long days of the short southern summer, from December to March, where air temperatures rarely exceed 6°C.[1] For the rest of the year the grass is covered by snow. To survive such extreme environmental conditions, hairgrass has evolved morphological and physiological features to cope with water stress and freezing temperatures. The bamboo *Neurolepis aristata* reaches 4,500 metres on the snowline of the Andes, while other grasses exploit the deserts of Africa, Asia and Australia, and coastlines worldwide. Geyser panic grass thrives in soils that exceed 50°C around hot springs in Yellowstone National Park, USA.[2] Other grasses survive on the toxic soils around British and Polish copper refineries.[3]

Besides the sheer number of grass species and the diversity of habitats they occupy, some grass species occur naturally at very high densities. Few flowering plant species dominate landscapes based on sheer numbers of individuals as effectively as grasses. Vast tracts of the steppes of Central Asia and the prairies of North America are covered with just a few grass species. Size variation between species is also dramatic. The European early sand-grass is an annual that may flower when it is only about 1.5 centimetres tall, while bamboos may be tens of metres tall and flower only once in their 120-year life span.

Grass Forms

Grasses are highly recognizable in landscapes but were dismissed by the lexicographer Samuel Johnson, a man with interest in neither landscape nor natural history, as 'a blade of grass is always a blade of grass, whether in one country or another'.[4] Johnson, like many people, had a limited appreciation of grass diversity.

Stereotypical grasses have narrow, green, ribbon-like, parallel-veined leaves. During the spring and summer they produce distinctive, often elaborate and delicate groups of flowers (inflorescences). Individual grass flowers are not usually showy, and if recognized at all they are revealed by short-lived anthers hanging from inflorescences. Traditionally, grasses have been grouped in the Glumiflorae, not because of their dull, insignificant flowers, but because of the numerous papery scales that surround the flowers. Despite the ease of recognition of grasses and their apparent simplicity, a complex vocabulary to describe them has been developed and refined by agrostologists (scientists who study grasses). This is not the place to explore such vocabulary in detail, but it is necessary to understand a little of the terminology before we proceed much further into the realms of grass biology.

Flowers of the tropical Dutch grass, showing the orange anthers and black stigmas.

Roots and bud of
a Brazilian bamboo.

Grasses are usually annual, biennial or perennial, that is they germinate, flower and produce seed in one year, two years or every year. Annuals die after one year; exceptionally, some grasses that are usually perennial only live for one year. Grasses produce vegetative and flowering shoots; vegetative shoots (tillers) are usually produced by biennial and perennial grasses, while annual grasses mainly produce flowering shoots. A typical grass culm (stem) looks like a piece of thin bamboo, and is usually a hollow cylinder with prominent, solid nodes at the points where the leaves arise. Grass leaves are arranged alternately, on either side of the culm, and are divided into two specific parts, the sheath which surrounds the culm and the blade which is free from the culm. At the junction of the sheath and the blade there is usually a ring of hairs or a membrane called the ligule. The ligule is rather like a seal and is thought to protect the developing leaf, by

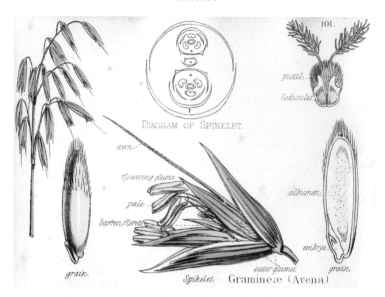

Morphology of the oat flower, as illustrated by Walter Fitch in a
19th-century botany teaching manual.

excluding water and harmful spores or secreting lubricants to aid the
growth of the developing shoot.[5] The simplicity of the basic plan belies
the enormous variation in grass leaves. For example, the leaves of
Spartochloa scirpoidea, from semi-arid areas in southwestern Australia,
lack a blade; the leaf blades of the northern-temperate forage red fescue are needle-like; and the blades of the Ecuadorian bamboo *Neurolepis
elata* can be up to 5 metres long and 30 centimetres wide. *Hygrochloa
aquatica* may produce spongy leaf sheaths that help the grass to float in
the swamps of Western Australia.

The grass inflorescence is made up of structures called spikelets.
Each spikelet is defined by two basal scales called glumes, and may
contain one or more florets. In turn, each floret is defined by two
papery scales, the lemma and palea. Inside these scales there are
usually two minute, fleshy, globular structures (lodicules), three male
stamens (androecium) and the female gynoecium.

In 1814, in the report of his botanical exploration of Australia as
part of Matthew Flinders's crew on the *Investigator*, the Scottish botanist
Robert Brown discussed grass biology. He concluded that the grass

spikelet was a branched structure where all the stalks were contracted and individual flowers were crowded together. Furthermore, Brown equated the lemma and palea with a typical flower's calyx, and the lodicules with its corolla.[6] In the early twenty-first century detailed investigations of the genes involved in the development of grass flowers drew identical conclusions.[7] Therefore, although the grass flower is superficially odd, it bears many similarities to more familiar flowers.

When the lodicules of the floret expand they force the lemma and palea apart, the two or three feathery styles and stamens are exposed, and pollination may take place. The vast majority of grasses are wind pollinated but some are insect pollinated. In some species florets may be sterile or modified to form bristles. In others glumes and lemmas may bear bristles, spines, or elaborate arms and hooks. Spikelets

Mature fruits of bur grass are covered in tough spines to aid inadvertent dispersal by animals.

are aggregated into numerous forms of inflorescences, for example the spike-like inflorescence of barley, the paniculate inflorescence of meadow grass and the hand-like inflorescence of crabgrass. In the Andean grass *Aciachne acicularis*, the entire inflorescence is a single, solitary spikelet, while the inflorescence of tropical American arrow grass is a panicle, up to 2 metres high, of several million spikelets. Modifying the basic spikelet and inflorescence form means that even closely related grasses may appear startlingly different, for example maize and its wild relative teosinte.

Grass fruits (grains or caryopses) are usually single seeded, dry and with the seed coat fused to the fruit wall. However, the Indo-Burmese pear bamboo produces a fleshy fruit every half century that is about the size and shape of a small avocado. Fruits of wild grasses, which soon fall off the parent plant, are often protected by lemmas and paleas that remain firmly attached to the outside of the grain. Within a grass grain there is a well-developed embryo and starchy endosperm (storage tissue). The endosperm is surrounded by the aleurone layer, which during germination releases enzymes to break down the grain's energy reserves (starch). The grass embryo comprises an immature shoot and root, each surrounded by a protective sheath, and the scutellum, a structure rather like a mammalian placenta, which during germination absorbs nutrients from the endosperm and transports them to the growing seedling.

The Names of Grasses

Children revel in polysyllabic dinosaur names, but when faced with scientific names adults are often left cold. Familiar complaints are that the names are too difficult to pronounce and remember, closely followed by a plea for common names. Scientific names promote international communication; they are a means to transmit information. It is important that everyone should use the same name for the same thing. It does not matter what you call wheat as long as my concept of wheat is the same as yours. Consider the confusion and embarrassment if different people used different names for wheat – for example, my wheat is your prune, or her rice or his rubber tree.

A scientific name aims at achieving stability, is applied unambiguously and is understood across language barriers. Common names do not enjoy such uniformity or international recognition; instead they reflect the cultures, traditions, beliefs and prejudices of different peoples. The word 'grass' is used indiscriminately in common names, or it is used to refer to herbs with longish, narrow leaves, for example grass of Parnassus, knotgrass, scorpion-grass and sea-grass. Many plants, especially disregarded ones such as grasses, lack traditional common names. In the official British list of plant common names a widely distributed European grass is known as smooth meadow-grass. In other parts of Europe this grass is called *pâturin des prés* (France), *capim-do-campo* (Portugal), *grama de prados* (Spanish) and *Wiesen-Rispengras* (Germany). The species was introduced into the United States in the early 1600s, but by the late nineteenth century it had become known as Kentucky bluegrass, and Senator John Ingalls waxed lyrical, with local pride, about the importance of this special Kentucky forage grass. The Russian name for the grass (*Мятлик луговой*) is simply a translation of the grass's scientific name, *Poa pratensis*.

Poa pratensis was formally named in 1753 by the Swedish naturalist Carolus Linnaeus. Before Linnaeus named it this grass sported a multitude of complex phrase names, including *Gramen pratense paniculatum majus, latiore folio* (the large-panicled meadow grass with broad leaves) and *Poa spiculis ovatis compressis muticus* (the grass with ovate, flattened, pointed spikes). Linnaeus's innovation was the consistent application of a simple binomial naming system, which today is governed by the International Code of Botanical Nomenclature. The first name, *Poa* (from the Greek meaning 'grass'), is the genus name and refers to a group of more than 500 species. The second word, *pratensis* (meaning 'of the meadow'), uniquely identifies a particular species. Below the level of the species there are also subspecies, varieties and forms. Despite the code, some species have numerous scientific names (synonyms), in addition to the accepted name, because of the discovery of earlier valid

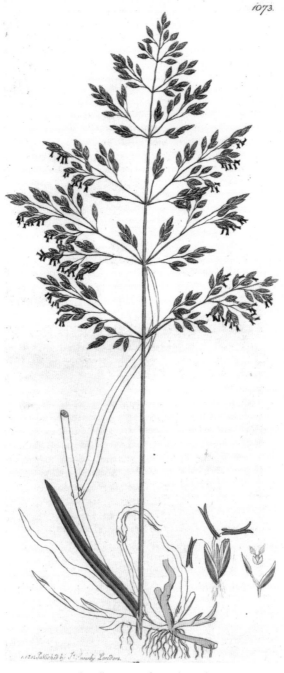

James Sowerby's illustration of smooth meadow grass, 1802.

names or due to new research. The correct identification and application of names for grasses that have been cultivated for hundreds of years is often difficult. Consequently, unambiguous association of the common name for a cultivated plant and its scientific name may not be possible. Today, the naming of cultivars produced by selection and breeding is governed by the International Code of Nomenclature for Cultivated Plants.

Because of the economic importance of grasses and their long cultivation history, agrostologists are reluctant to make formal name changes unless absolutely necessary. Despite my defence of scientific names, common names are used in this book where possible; a complete list of their scientific equivalents is given in the Appendix.

Grasses and the Tree of Life

The grasses belong to a large group of the flowering plants called the monocotyledons, which includes other familiar plants such as orchids, tulips, crocuses, palms and lilies. Monocotyledons are usually herbs (although some are tree-like), with flower parts arranged in threes, leaves with parallel veins and only a single seed leaf (cotyledon). In the case of the grasses the cotyledon comprises the scutellum (equivalent to the leaf blade) and the coleoptile (equivalent to the leaf sheath). Monocotyledons were first recognized as a distinct group by the illustrious English naturalist John Ray in 1682, and the group's distinctiveness has survived the attention of late twentieth-century researchers using DNA sequences to investigate the evolutionary relationships of all the world's flowering plants.[8] About one-third of the 60,000 monocotyledons belong to the order Poales which, in addition to the grasses, includes the sedges, pineapples, rushes and pipeweeds.

DNA sequences encode the genes that make organisms, and hold within their structure clues to evolutionary relationships. DNA may contain thousands of characters suitable for evolutionary investigation, far more than are available from morphology, anatomy or chemistry. Furthermore, DNA offers the possibility of being able to compare grasses that superficially appear very different. The trick is to find sequences that evolve at rates appropriate for the problem being investigated. If a sequence evolves too rapidly ancient relationships will be erased; if a sequence evolves too slowly recent relationships will be invisible. Using pieces of DNA found in the photosynthetic powerhouses of plant cells (chloroplasts), the patterns of relationships among families of the Poales have been determined in the past two decades.[9]

Within the Poales, the closest living relatives of the grasses belong to two tiny families. One family, the Ecdeiocoleaceae, comprises three species restricted to the infertile soils of the arid parts of southwestern Australia. The other family, the Joinvilleaceae, contains only two species, distributed from the Malay Peninsula to the Pacific Islands. Clues to the relationship between the Joinvilleaceae and the grasses came from morphological studies, but the importance of the Ecdeiocoleaceae was only recognized when DNA sequences were investigated.[10]

The more than 11,000 species of the Poaceae are split into twelve subfamilies, ranging in size from nearly 4,000 species to fewer than five.[11] Many of these subfamilies have been recognized for centuries; for example, at the start of the nineteenth century the botanist Robert Brown identified the two largest subfamilies, Pooideae (*c.* 3,800 species, including wheat, barley and oats) and Panicoideae (*c.* 3,200 species, including maize and sorghum), based on the appearance of the spikelet.[12] In the late 1990s an international group of scientists combined efforts to investigate the grass evolutionary tree using chloroplast DNA.[13]

The general picture that has emerged from these investigations is one of two major groups (clades) forming the core of the grasses. The BEP clade comprises the bamboo subfamily (Bambusoideae; *c.* 1,500 species), the rice subfamily (Ehrhartoideae; *c.* 100 species) and the wheat-barley subfamily (Pooideae; *c.* 3,800 species). The PACMAD clade contains the maize-sorghum subfamily (Panicoideae; *c.* 3,200 species), the three-awn grass subfamily (Aristidoideae; *c.* 350 species), the lovegrass subfamily (Chloroideae; *c.* 1,600 species), the resurrection grass subfamily (Micrairoideae; *c.* 190 species), the reed subfamily (Arundinoideae; *c.* 45 species) and the heath grass subfamily

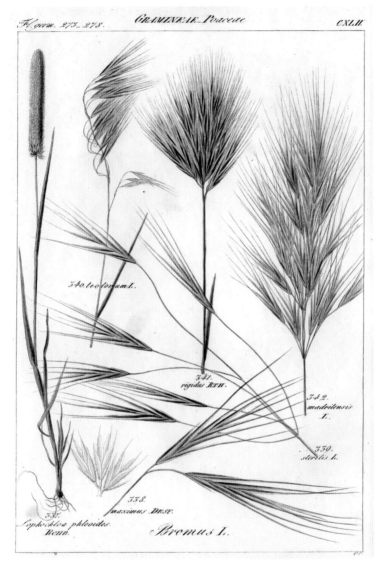

Selection of northern European grasses, from Reichenbach's *Icones Florae Germanicae et Helveticae, Agrostographia Germanica* (1850).

English earthenware tile handpainted by Japanese artists with
bamboo and flying birds, late 18th century.

(Danthonioideae; *c.* 280 species). Outside the core grass groups there
are three subfamilies, which comprise fewer than 30 species of perennial, broadleaved tropical forest grasses. One grass is basal to all other
grasses, and is the sole member of the appropriately named genus
Anomochloa ('unusual grass'). *Anomochloa* is restricted to the coastal
Atlantic forests of Bahia in northeast Brazil and was first described in
1851. Cultivated in European botanic gardens, this grass was unknown
in the wild until it was rediscovered by the Argentian botanist Cleofé
Calderón in 1976.[14] When *Anomochloa* was first discovered Atlantic
forest covered approximately 15 per cent of Brazilian territory; today
Atlantic forest covers only about 1.8 per cent of Brazil. Furthermore,
Anomochloa is known from only two small populations, both of which are
outside any formal protection.[15] *Anomochloa* is unusual among grasses

Anomochloa marantoidea, the most basal living grass, as illustrated by Walter Fitch in 1862.

in lacking true spikelets, and having four stamens rather than the usual three, as well as a stalked leaf blade like some bamboos.

Grasses, Geology and Diversity

Until recently a familiar botanical mantra was 'dinosaurs did not eat grass'; the family was thought to have diversified long after the dinosaurs had become extinct. The earliest grass records appeared to occur for the first time in the fossil pollen record of the South American and

African Paleocene (60 and 55 million years ago) and fossil spikelets are known from the Palaeocene–Eocene boundary (*c.* 55 million years ago); the non-bird-like dinosaurs were extinct by the Late Cretaceous (67 to 65 million years ago). However, in 2005 a group of Indian palaeontologists surprised botanists by revealing that fossilized Indian dinosaur dung (coprolites) contained grass remains. The remains were phytoliths, the distinctive grains of silica produced by grasses, apparently as a protection against grazers. Indeed, so abundant are phytoliths in grasses that glass, a silica-rich non-crystalline solid, is often reported to have been found in the ashes of haystack fires. For example, in 1961 in Western Australia, a 325-tonne haystack burned and yielded 16 tonnes of silica glass.[16] Importantly, the dinosaur-dung phytoliths were not those characteristic of primitive grass subfamilies but those found in the BEP clade. Not only were grasses present in the Cretaceous, but they had diversified.[17]

If one assumes that particular numbers of mutations occur every one million years in a DNA sequence, by counting the number of mutations between pairs of grass species it is possible to determine how long ago they shared a common ancestor. That is, with each tick of the molecular clock, another mutation occurs in a piece of DNA. To investigate DNA changes millions of years ago it is necessary to have sequences where the molecular clock ticks slowly and regularly. To calibrate the tick, fossils are crucial since they can fix dates for particular grass groups. For example, fossil data implies that the BEP and PACMAD clades diversified in the last 70 million years. Thus, the rate at which the grass clock ticks may be determined. Analysis of molecular data implies that the BEP and PACMAD clades originated 80 to 85 million years ago and grasses emerged some 90 million years ago.

More controversial, and surprising, was the report in 2004 of a spikelet and leaf identified as a subfamily Pooideae fossil trapped in Burmese amber that was some 100 million years old.[18] Since the fossil is from a derived grass group, if confirmed, the Poaceae must be at

opposite: Variegated giant reed leaf illustrating the parallel leaf venation typical of grasses.

least twice as old as any previous estimates. Evolutionary trees show that some of the most primitive grasses are found in areas that were once part of the geological supercontinent Gondwana. In contrast, the amber deposits are from an area that was part of the other supercontinent, Laurasia. Despite our new understanding of grass evolution, discrepancies among sources of evidence show that much detailed research remains to be done.

Since the grasses are so prominent on the planet, questions naturally arise as to why they are so ecologically successful and evolutionarily diverse. Grasses share features such as wind pollination, highly reduced flowers and silica accumulation with other, less diverse members of the Poales. Consequently, these shared features are unlikely to hold the key to the success and diversity of the grasses. The first grasses appear to have been plants of forest shade, for example *Anomochloa* and the bamboos. Grasses persisted in the forest for millions of years but did not diversify much. Only when they escaped the confines of the forest and started to occupy drier, more open areas did they start to diversify. In the temperate regions it was the subfamily Pooideae of the BEP clade that diversified. In the tropics and subtropics the subfamilies Panicoideae and Chloroideae of the PACMAD clade diversified.

In 1890 the Swiss plant anatomist and physiologist Simon Schwendener reported a distinct anatomical difference between the leaves of grasses in the subfamilies Pooideae and Panicoideae. Members of the latter subfamily had narrowly spaced veins running through their leaves that were surrounded by rings of large cells (the bundle sheath). This particular arrangement of cells, known as Kranz anatomy, is associated with a special type of photosynthesis common in the Panicoideae but absent from the Pooideae.

In most plants photosynthesis, the biochemical process by which carbon dioxide and water are converted into sugars through the action of sunlight, is mediated through the 'Jekyll and Hyde' enzyme Ribulose bisphosphate carboxylase oxygenase (RuBisCO). As Jekyll, RuBisCO adds carbon dioxide to a sugar containing five carbon atoms to produce two three-carbon molecules, which eventually

Selection of northern European grasses from Reichenbach's
Icones Florae Germanicae et Helveticae, Agrostographia Germanica (1850).

produces sugars and starch. This is C_3 photosynthesis and is typical of grasses in tropical and temperate areas with access to moderate amounts of water, sunlight and carbon dioxide.

As temperatures or water stresses increase, the Hyde-side of RuBisCO emerges. Instead of adding more carbon dioxide to the five-carbon sugar, oxygen is added, a process called photorespiration. Photorespiration reduces the efficiency of photosynthesis. To overcome the disadvantages of photorespiration, plants have developed different strategies to survive in dry, hot environments. Some grasses have evolved a biochemical carbon pump at the start of C_3 photosynthesis that keeps carbon dioxide levels high. This process is C_4 photosynthesis. At night, in the bundle sheath cells, carbon dioxide is converted to molecules containing four carbon atoms. During the day these compounds are transported into other cells, where carbon dioxide is released and C_3 photosynthesis takes place.

C_4 grasses dominate the North American prairies, African grasslands and South American llanos and *cerrado*. At least three different sorts of C_4 photosynthesis have evolved on 22–24 separate occasions across the grass evolutionary tree. In fact, 46 per cent of all grasses are C_4, which includes important crops such as maize and sugar cane. The earliest leaf fragments that can confidently be described as C_4 are about 12.5 million years old, but studies based on the application of a molecular clock place the origin of C_4 photosynthesis in the grasses much earlier. The innovation of C_4 photosynthesis appears to have coincided with a shift from the tropical forest habitats to tropical woodlands and savannahs, where water was at a premium.[19]

Native grasslands are found on all continents, and develop where there are periodic droughts, frequent fires or extensive grazing. Grasslands fostered the evolution of large herbivores, were the cradle of human evolution and have become the granaries of the world.

two

Roaming the World

❧❦❧

I am a voyager and a seaman; that is, a liar and a stupid fellow, in the eyes of that class of indolent haughty writers, who . . . confine nature within the limits of their own invention. This way of proceeding appears very singular and inconceivable, on the part of persons who have observed nothing themselves, and only write and reason upon the observations which they have borrowed from those same travellers in whom they deny the faculty of seeing and thinking.

LOUIS-ANTOINE DE BOUGAINVILLE in John Forster,
A Voyage Around the World (1772)

Widely acknowledged as the first detailed naturalistic representation of a community of wild plants, Albrecht Dürer's *Das grosse Rasenstück* shows a sod of German meadow complete with grasses and other herbs. However, most northern European grasslands are products of human deforestation and subsequent management, as artificial as the parklands inspired by the gardener Capability Brown in eighteenth-century England. The planet's natural grasslands, which cover about one-quarter of its land area, are usually found where there are periodic droughts, frequent fires and extensive grazing, for example on the North American Great Plains, Eurasian steppes, southern African veld, East African savannah, and South American pampas and *cerrado*. However, some grasslands, such as the Pantanal in western Brazil and the Everglades in the southeastern United States, are periodically flooded, while others, in the upper Amazon, are vast floating meadows, grazed by manatees.

The East African grasslands were the crucible of our evolution, out of which we emerged to colonize almost the entire planet.[1] In pre-Columbian South America the *Caminho do Peabiru* ('path of crushed grass'), through the grasslands of southern Brazil, was maintained for centuries by Amerindians as a link between the Andes and the Brazilian coast.[2] In the thirteenth century Ghengis Khan used Central Asian grasslands as a route to create an empire that eventually stretched from the Sea of Japan to eastern Europe.[3] Genetic evidence for the spread of the Mongol hordes across the steppe is found in today's Mongol, Kazakh and southern Siberian populations; 8 per cent of the region's men carry a mutation that appears to have originated in Mongolia about one millennium ago.[4] During the twentieth century the *voortreker* and cowboy, so strongly associated with the veld and American prairies of the previous century, were cultural, often highly romanticized icons of exploration, defiance and man's conquest of nature, both icons having swept aside the indigenous cultures of their respective lands. However, grasslands are more than the

Hans Hoffman's *A Small Piece of Turf* (1574), which is reminiscent of Dürer's *Das grosse Rasenstück* (1503).

28

Meadows of floating grasses form extensive islands in the black water
regions of Amazonia.

surfaces upon which evolutionary and cultural events in human history unfold. They are biological powerhouses supporting diverse
communities of many different types of plant and animal, above and
below their surfaces. Beneath the 'beauty and the quiet calm' of a
grassland,[5] a centuries-old biological war is waged annually.

Human Reactions to Grasslands

The term 'grassland' belies the ecological complexity and diversity
of these communities. Grasslands, spread across the world's climatic regions, are often hemmed in by geography and climate and vary
dramatically in their characteristics. Few people come to grassland landscapes with an open mind; the impressions produced depend upon the
expectations and interests of the observer. Consequently, writers and
explorers have emphasized different aspects of these lands. In South
America the *cerrado* occupies a broad expanse of nutrient-poor,
aluminium-rich, heavily leached soils in the highland plateau of
the continental centre. The Amazon forest is found to the north,
the Andes to the west and the Brazilian coastal forest to the east. In

the south the *cerrado* mingles with the grasslands of southern, temperate South America. In an influential book on Brazilian vegetation, the Brazilian botanist Aylthon Joly, a man fascinated by Brazil's coastal forest, entitled one of the chapters 'the monotonous *cerrado*' because he thought it all looked the same.

In South and East Africa the quantity of game that passed before the guns of nineteenth-century explorers in savannah grasslands was of particular note:

> a great treeless plain covered with a close and succulent coating of grass quite indistinguishable from the pasture of more temperate climates . . . the country spread out before us in gently waving plains diversified by low, rounded ridges, small humpy hills or volcanic cones . . . great herds of buffalo . . . enormous numbers of the harmless but fierce-looking wildebeest continue their grazing . . . companies of that loveliest of all large game, the zebra, conspicuous in their beautiful striped skin . . . the great, unwieldy rhinoceros, with horns stuck on their noses in a most offensive and pugnacious manner . . . ostriches are scudding away out of reach of danger, defying pursuit, and too wary for the stalker . . . herds of hartebeest . . . the graceful pallah springing into mid-air . . . the dignified waterbuck.[6]

The North American prairies, which cover an area about five times that of France, are bounded to the west by the deserts of the Rocky Mountains and to the east by the woodlands of the Appalachians, and drained by the Mississippi River. When explorers first came into contact with the prairies, the detachment of even the most seasoned traveller evaporated. The nineteenth-century botanist Edwin James was fulsome:

> our path lay through extensive and fertile meadows, stretching away to the distant horizon, and bounded sometimes by

Cerrado landscape in the Brazilian state of Goiás.

the verge of the sky, and sometimes by the margin of a forest. The elk, the deer, and the bison, the indigenous inhabitants of these delightful meadows, had been long since been driven away by the incursions of the white settlers, scattered at remote intervals on the borders of the forests. The dense and uniform growth of grass had risen untrodden and uncropped, and was now waving with ceaseless undulations, as the wind swept lightly over the surface of the plain.[7]

The steppe, a grassland ribbon extending from the Black Sea in the west to China in the east, is bounded by coniferous forests in the north and the deserts and mountains of Central Asia in the south. The duality of the Russian steppe in the height of summer was captured by Anton Chekhov in his novella *The Steppe* (1888). Desolate and torpid during the day,

After Michel Bouquet, *Cabanes dans les steppes*, 19th-century lithograph.

the grass drooped, everything living was hushed . . . the sky, which seems terribly deep and transparent in the steppes, where there are no woods or high hills, seemed now endless, petrified with dreariness' yet 'in the July nights . . . as soon as the sun goes down and the darkness enfolds the earth, the day's weariness is forgotten, everything is forgiven, and the steppe breathes a light sigh from its broad bosom. As though because the grass cannot see in the dark that it has grown old, a gay youthful twitter rises up from it, such as is not heard by day.[8]

The World's Grasslands

Ongoing debates suggest that grasses evolved up to 100 million years ago and that grasslands began to emerge as early as 34 million years ago. However, it was not until five to twelve million years ago that grass-dominated communities (grasslands) spread and diversified across the globe.[9] The distribution of the world's grasslands involves inter-actions of climate, soil and disturbance. In the face of such complexities, scientists have proposed many systems to name grasslands. Broadly and simplistically, grasslands can be grouped into tropical and subtropical savannahs (grasslands with scattered trees), tropical and subtropical montane grasslands (páramo) and treeless temperate grasslands. Climatic grasslands occur in areas of strong seasonality. The cold winters and hot summers of the North American prairies, and the distinct wet and prolonged dry seasons of East African savannahs, are examples of climatic grasslands.

In contrast, edaphic grasslands form when soil properties limit the growth of plants. Soils are complex mixtures of sand, clay and the remains of dead plants (humus). Sand improves soil drainage and aeration but limits fertility, while high soil clay content impedes drainage making soils heavy. Humus leavens the mix; it is like an electrically charged sponge that absorbs water and traps important plant nutrients. Water and nutrients are held, by humus, at different soil levels by the balance of evaporation and rainfall. If rainfall exceeds evaporation, humus becomes waterlogged, nutrients are leached beyond the reach of plant roots and soil acidity increases. If evaporation exceeds rainfall, humus acts as a wick, dragging nutrients (perhaps to toxic levels) from the soil depths, and increasing salinity and alkalinity. Grasses are found growing on all soil types, but only a limited range of soils is capable of supporting grasslands. The llanos of Venezuela and Colombia are treeless savannahs maintained by the annual flooding of the rivers Orinoco and Arauca. In contrast, the treeless savannahs of the African Serengeti are products of nutrient-poor quartzite soils and disturbance.

Disturbance plays a major role in so-called derived grasslands since it tends to discourage tree growth. Disturbance may be natural or anthropogenic, and is primarily associated with fire and grazing. For example, East African woodlands can be transformed into savannah when elephants destroy trees and open areas to invasion by grasses.[10] Other grazers then prevent woodland regeneration by eliminating tree seedlings. Only trees and shrubs such as thorny acacias, which are capable of coping with heavy grazing, can establish themselves, leading to the formation of acacia savannah.

Grasslands are diverse plant communities, where mats of stems and roots bind friable soils and protect them from water and wind erosion.

African savannah, with a mixture of grasses and trees, feeds a diverse array of different grazers and browsers.

However, life for most grassland plants is tough. Soil water may be limited, since grasses and other plants compete within and among themselves. Grazers place grassland communities under constant pressure, and fires may be frequent. In temperate and high-altitude grasslands, species must be adapted to cold, wet conditions for at least part of the year, although during the summer months daily temperatures may range over 40°C. In tropical and subtropical regions, adaptations to seasonally hot, dry conditions are essential.

Water

Water is fundamental to plant life; all plants need water to grow and reproduce. Grasses are adept at coping with changes in water availability. Since grass roots tend to grow to the depth of the water reserves, average grass height is a good indicator of available water. Apparently dead, straw-yellow grasses of African and South American savannahs in the dry season, and European lawns in the height of summer, are transformed with the arrival of the rains. Within days, the grasses produce new shoots and a green haze covers the ground.

In these cases water is seasonally limited. Water may also be limited daily (diurnally) because of climate, or continually limited because of the numbers of plants competing for it. To move water from the soil to their leaves, through an intricate vascular system, plants must lose water from their leaves, that is they transpire. The strategies adopted by plants to cope with the dilemma of having to lose water in order to acquire it involve minimizing water loss from the leaves and maximizing water uptake from the soil.

The most obvious reason for water stress is that there is little water available. More subtle examples of water stress are seen in plants growing in damp soils in very windy environments. Under these conditions plants are in danger of drying out, since high winds increase transpiration rates. Such physiological drought is also associated with low-temperature environments, such as páramo, and high transpiration during sunny periods. Many grasses have evolved morphological, physiological and chemical strategies to cope with temporary drought by short-term acclimatization and long-term adaptation.

One of the most dramatic adaptations for coping with water stress was the evolution of C_4 photosynthesis and the rapid ecological dominance of the grasses some three to eight million years ago. The parallel evolution of C_4 in many different grass lineages is often considered to be an adaptation to arid environments or a change in atmospheric carbon dioxide concentration. However, C_4 photosynthesis evolved before grasses emerged from the forests to colonize more arid habitats.[11] Not only are C_4 grasses more efficient at using water than C_3 grasses; they are also more nitrogen efficient and better able to use light.

Tussock formation is another strategy adopted by many grasses, such as reedgrasses in the South American páramo and the feather grasses in the Eurasian steppe, as a means of protection from desiccation, and in some cases the risk of freezing. Dense tufts, where dead leaves are retained and decay on the grass, insulate young leaves from low temperatures, high insolation and evaporation. Such grasses may also have rigid leaves that roll up when placed under water stress, as in the sand dune grass, marram. By rolling up, the surface area of a grass leaf is reduced, the leaf pores (stomata) are protected and water loss is minimized. Long, rolled leaves can also be important for water harvesting. The central Namib Desert is an extreme environment for life; rains are rare and diurnal temperatures fluctuate widely. However, some plants and animals have evolved to take advantage of the desert's regular fogs. The long, upright, curled leaves of bushman grass intercept water droplets in the fog. On the leaf surfaces water droplets coalesce, eventually rolling down the leaf to the grass's base, where they are absorbed by the extensive root network on the desert surface.[12]

In grasslands the vast majority of grasses are perennials, although some annual grasses take advantage of transient gaps in plant cover. Tall, deep-rooted perennials draw on the deepest water reserves. Smaller perennials flower early in the year and complete their life cycles before surface layers have dried up. Annuals are opportunists, germinating, growing, flowering and dropping seed in one short season; the seeds remain dormant in the soil. In North America, to the east of the Mississippi, the so-called tall-grass prairie is dominated by grasses such as big bluestem and switchgrass. Big bluestem, an important forage grass of the Mississippi Valley, can reach 2 metres in height. As one travels further west short-grass prairie, dominated by buffalo grass, appears. Buffalo-grass, which reaches about 20 centimetres in height, is also an important fodder plant, especially during the winter; sods of it were used to make the houses of early prairie settlers. Between the extremes are mixed-grass prairies.

We are all familiar with the idea that plants grow to different heights and take advantage of different light levels above ground. Similarly, deep, highly branched root systems can take advantage of water resources at different depths in the soil. For example, in the prairies, June grass and little bluestem, which reach heights of about 60 centimetres and 1.5 metres respectively, have root systems that reach similar depths, whilst some of the prairie legumes and daisies may extend their roots to 5 metres below the soil surface. Furthermore,

Parched savannah landscape in central Brazil.

an individual grass may exploit more than 3,000 litres of soil. Grasses may also respond to drought by changing their chemistry, becoming coarser and less palatable to grazers as the season progresses. Hence grazers move to deeper rooted, 'sweeter' species. The underground parts of the grasses are also food stores for long dormant periods and allow grasses to grow rapidly with the arrival of spring or the rains.

Too much water can be as much of a problem for grasses as too little water. The primary problem of waterlogging is anoxia, since plant roots need oxygen to survive. Grasses growing in waterlogged conditions, such as rice and floating sweet grass, therefore show morpho - logical and physiological adaptations for growing in conditions of low oxygen. For example, cavities in the stems and leaves allow air to get to the roots, or the grasses float on the water's surface. The grasses of woodlands and forests are poorly adapted to both drought and flooding. Furthermore, the evolution of cold tolerance in some lineages of C_3 grasses is also likely to have been important in shaping grasslands across the globe.[13]

Grazers

Buds are found at the bases of grasses, and when damaged grasses readily produce vegetative shoots. The perennial grasses may be divided into three broad groups, clumpers, creepers and tunnellers, depending on how they grow and protect their buds; without buds grasses stop growing. Clumpers are the tussock-forming grasses, such as tufted hairgrass, where the buds are crowded together and the plants slowly grow sideways. Creepers such as creeping bent produce bud-covered, above-ground horizontal stems (stolons). In contrast, tunnellers like smooth meadow grass have bud-covered, below-ground horizontal stems (rhizomes). Furthermore, grass leaves have intercalary meristems, meaning that they will continue to grow even if the leaf tip is removed. Due to the positions of these growing points grasses can be regularly grazed or mown without suffering severe damage. Indeed, grazing may stimulate grass growth. However, with too much grazing grasses become stunted and poorly rooted. Eventually they die, leaving gaps that are either recolonized or invaded by weeds, especially when temperatures are too low for grass seed to germinate. In extreme circumstances the gaps become foci for soil erosion.

The main grazers of grasses are large and often charismatic vertebrates such as horses, camels, cows and elephants, small vertebrates such as rodents, rabbits and hares, and invertebrates such as insects and molluscs. The first ungulates (hoofed mammals), which were probably browsers (predominantly non-grass herbivores), appeared about 55 million years ago, while the first true grazers (predominantly grass feeders) are only about ten million years old.[14] As climates changed and grasslands spread, the diversity of browsing mammals decreased and that of grazing mammals increased.

The evolution of the modern horse appears to parallel this story. As North American woodlands gave way to the prairies, three-toed horses that were well adapted to moving in woodlands gave way to single-toed horses that were well adapted for life on the plains.[15] Modern horses spread rapidly across the Old World soon after their

Mongolian grass.

evolution, between four and seven million years ago, but became extinct in the Americas. Modern horses were reintroduced to the Americas by Christopher Columbus in 1493, were important in Hernán Cortés's conquest of Mexico and eventually formed feral populations in the prairie homelands of their distant ancestors.

Horse domestication was a key cultural event in human history and appears to have occurred in the Eurasian steppes about 6,000 years ago.[16] Horses made people mobile and horse culture spread. Powered by grass, domesticated horses were sufficiently adaptable to be used for transportation, agricultural work and warfare, as well as for food. Adapted to the rigours of life on the Eurasian steppes, horses were central to the rise and establishment of the Mongol Empire. They gave Ghengis Khan and his followers speed and flexibility, while other grazers, such as camels, cattle, sheep and goats, enabled the growing empire to feed itself and establish trade routes to link its boundaries.

Grasses are well equipped with physical grazing protection in the form of phytoliths, distinctive grains of silica found inside cells. Phytoliths can be viewed as adaptations to herbivory, where the silica abrades an animal's teeth, mandibles or radulae. Conversely, the evolution of grinding molars and premolars in ungulate grazers and browsers may be a response to increased silica in the diet. Thus, whether phytoliths evolved as adaptations to grazing or were incidentally beneficial has been the subject of considerable academic discussion.[17] When compared with other grassland plant families, such as the legumes and daisies, grasses have few of the chemical defences that are associated with grazing protection.

The effects of grazers on grasses and grasslands may be seen by considering bison behaviour.[18] The bison is the largest North American mammal and the dominant grazer of the prairies. Before the arrival of Europeans it is estimated that there were 30 to 60 million head, but wholesale slaughter in the mid-nineteenth century diminished numbers to a few thousand. Today, bison numbers have risen, causing tensions among diverse groups of prairie users.[19] Bison have strong preferences for grasses, leading to the formation of closely cropped grazing lawns. In cropped areas grasses tend to be more nutritious than in other areas. Smaller grazing patches are also formed, but as these become dominated by non-grasses bison move to new grazing grounds. Consequently, grazing patches migrate across the prairie landscapes. Other bison behaviour, such as trampling, wallowing, defecation, urination and death, changes the distributions of grasses and other plants, adding to overall prairie heterogeneity. Furthermore, bison have a preference for grazing in areas that have been burned.

Fire

At the end of March 1805, William Clark, on his epic journey through the grasslands of the United States with Meriwether Lewis, reported that

> the Plains are on fire on both Sides of the river it is common
> for the indians to Set those Plains on fire near their village for

Fire is important for grassland ecology but, during tropical dry seasons,
is a threat to people living in areas surrounded by grassland.

the advantage of early Grass for the hors & as an inducement
to the Buffalow to visit them.[20]

Humans had learned to make fire 30–40 millennia earlier, and
used it to harvest and cook their food, clear land, enrich soil, and
drive and herd game, and even as a weapon.[21] However, Prometheus's
gift was important for grassland ecology and evolution long before
humans were a significant part of the planet's fauna.[22] Some grasslands, for example those of South Africa, Australia and North America,
are maintained by frequent, recurrent fires; without the fires, woodland takes over. Fire is less important for grassland maintenance in
areas where tree establishment is unlikely, for example where aridity
is high, such as the steppes, or where temperature is low, such as
the páramo.

Fire, a chemical chain reaction requiring fuel, oxygen and heat, is
an important part of the disturbance regime of grassland ecosystems.
Ecologically, fire is chemical grazing. During dormant periods, dry

seasons and periodic droughts, fuel in the form of dead leaves and stems accumulates, while lightning strikes provide the necessary sparks. On the prairies of Dakota and Montana in the United States, it has been estimated that between six and 92 lightning strikes occur annually in an area approximately half the size of Wales.[23] With a little wind, convection currents soon establish themselves and fire spreads across a landscape. Fires range from the smouldering, slow-burning types to rapidly travelling infernos with flames metres high. The intensity of grassland fires depends on weather conditions, topography and fuel type, with temperatures ranging from less than 100°C to over 700°C. Fire temperature influences seed germination, bud resprouting, soil microbes and soil nutrients. Fire initially raises the temperature of the soil surface and removes living and dead plant material. After the fire there are high light levels, little competition from other plants and a warm, sterile, nutrient-rich ash in which seeds can germinate. However, there is loss of some nutrients, especially nitrogen and sulphur, and wind and water erosion increase until the soil surface is stabilized. Surface stabilization can start within days of a fire, as the first seeds germinate and perennials begin to resprout.

Unlike animals, the plants of grassland ecosystems cannot run away from fire. Some grassland plants are killed by fire and must recolonize burned areas. However, many grassland species are well adapted to protecting seeds and the buds of adults from the effects of fire. These are the pyrophytes, which require fire to stimulate flower - ing, fruit set or seed germination, and the pyrophiles, which obtain a competitive advantage over other plants when burned. Soil is an excellent insulator, and during a fire temperatures a few centimetres below the surface hardly rise. Consequently, seeds and buds of grasses and other herbs buried in the soil are protected from blazes. The recovery of grassland after fire appears to be at least as dependent on the size of the soil bud bank as the soil seed bank.[24] The accumulation of dead leaves around tightly packed growing points also acts as insulation. When the Ecuadorian páramo burns the upper leaves of *Calamagrostis* grass tussocks reach temperatures in excess of 500°C,

The sedge *Bulbostylis paradoxa* resprouting following a fire in the Brazilian *cerrado*.

but at the densely packed leaf bases, around the growing points, temperatures do not even reach 65°C.[25] In the case of the woody savannah plants, thick, corky bark protects dormant buds, and where there are regular fires, stem and buds are below ground.

Excluding fire in fire-prone grasslands encourages transformation to woodland or change in grass species composition. For example, in the Brazilian *cerrado* fire prevention can lead to African weedy grasses, such as *capim gordura* and *jaraguá* grass, outcompeting native species, since they photosynthesize and use nutrients more efficiently.[26] Increasing fire frequency also changes grassland species composition and transforms savannah grassland into treeless grassland.

Grassland Disappearance

We have destroyed and fragmented the world's natural grasslands to satisfy the food and accommodation needs of a continually expanding human population. Forests gave way to artificial grasslands in the wake of anthropogenic fire, while natural grasslands on easily ploughed soils soon disappeared as man learned to grow his own food. The

Brazilian *cerrado* cleared of native species, invaded by exotics
and now suffering from overgrazing by cattle.

transformation of grasslands on heavy alluvial soils had to await the development of animal-powered and eventually tractor-powered heavy ploughs. Many of the easily converted areas have now been transformed, so marginal areas, such as montane tropical grasslands, are being encroached upon. Today the North American prairies are an essential part of the global granary network. In the late 1940s Stalin dreamed of the European steppes feeding the Soviet people and implemented the soon-to-be-abandoned Great Plan for the Transformation of Nature,[27] yet the greatest current threat to the steppes is the discovery of oil and gas reserves.

The problem of continual grassland destruction is illustrated by the South American *cerrado*, the world's most diverse savannah. In Brazil *cerrado* covers an area about three and half times that of France, and contains about one-fifth of all Brazilian vascular plant species.[28] Estimates of the area of *cerrado* lost since 1500, when Europeans started to colonize Brazil, vary from 35 per cent to 80 per cent of the original area.[29] Despite the best efforts of botanists to emphasize the biological richness of the *cerrado*, the myth is maintained by those who would transform it into farmland that it is merely scrubland.[30] This is particularly problematic outside Brazil, where Amazonia still attracts the majority of public and political interest in environmental issues.

Ignoring the unknown consequences of species extinction, once natural grasslands are destroyed the environmental services they offer to humans will disappear. In the case of grasslands, soil protection is one obvious service at risk. In grasslands stripped of their grasses, dust devils carry away the topsoil during the dry months, and rain erodes soils during the wet months; the agricultural land created by grassland conversion gradually disappears. In the past 40 years approximately one-third of all agricultural land has been abandoned because of soil erosion.[31] Topsoils cannot readily be replaced; under agricultural conditions, it takes about half a millennium to form about 25 millimetres of soil. Furthermore, edaphic grasslands, on poor soils, can only be made temporarily productive by the addition of fertilizers and lime. Such temporary fixes are only economic as long as crop prices are high. Annual ploughing further destroys soil structure, leading to soil loss. The dustbowl of the 1930s in the United States of America is an iconic example of poor grassland management.

Plants superficially similar to grasses are common. Only two grasses are
in this piece of Brazilian grassland turf; the other grass-like species belong
to four unrelated families.

three

Disguising Grasses

ΚϽϹ

And the parched ground shall become a pool, and the thirsty land
spring of water: in the habitation of dragons, where each lay, shall
be grass with reeds and rushes.

ISAIAH 35:7

Rocks give drama to a landscape, streams provide serenity and
trees mood, while open areas, often apparently dominated
by grasses, leaven the mix. Furthermore, open areas created
by anthropogenic fire and grazing animals assert human mastery
over nature. The attention of the artist is drawn to the dramatic and
the showy, rather than the ecological glue. Rather like in a piece of
batik, the ecological warp and weft are overlooked in favour of the
vibrant pattern. Yet the ecological glue is not the same in all landscapes, and many plants that look like grasses are not true grasses.
In Europe, minute cliff-top sea thrift, sea plantain, marshland reed-
mace and bur-reeds may have the outward appearance of grasses.
In highland Brazil, tree lilies, daisies and pipeweeds are found scattered across friable, nutrient-poor, rocky soils and appear remarkably
similar to grass tussocks in the Scottish Highlands. Botanists acknowl-
edge such superficial similarities in scientific names like *graminifolius*
(grass-leaved) and *graminioides* (grass-like). Such names are given to
plants as diverse as legumes, daisies, mallows and even spurges and
insectivorous sundews, in addition to orchids, pipeweeds and palms.
However, in flower, none of these plants can possibly be confused

with grasses. The same is not true of two other plant families, the sedges (Cyperaceae) and rushes (Juncaceae); these are often mistaken for grasses, even in flower.

With their long, thin, parallel-veined leaves, grasses, sedges and rushes are superficially similar. Once considered to be rather distantly related, the DNAs of these plants reveal that they are closely related to each other.[1] By looking at stems and applying the familiar botanical mnemonic 'sedges have edges, rushes are round, and grasses, likes arses, have holes', rushes and sedges will rarely be confused with grasses. Sedge stems are usually triangular in cross section, whilst grasses and rushes have round stems that are usually hollow in the former and solid in the latter. Furthermore, sedges and rushes are generally plants of wet, often marginal areas and were significant components of the lands drained for cereal production in nineteenth-century Europe.

Rushes

Rushes belong to a small family of seven genera and about 400 species found predominantly in temperate and cold regions and on tropical mountains. Compared with the grasses, rushes are morphologically uniform; more than 70 per cent of rush species occur in one genus, *Juncus*. Most rushes are perennial, clump-forming plants of poorly drained soils, their extensive underground rhizome systems making them effective soil stabilizers. In parts of the Canary Islands, for example, sharp rush is used to stabilize the terraces surrounding fields carved from steep-sided volcanoes. Rush flowers are tiny, with the sepals and petals being reduced to dull-coloured segments. However, viewing a rush flower with a hand lens quickly reveals its similarity to a lily flower, which is unlike a grass flower.

Humans have found few uses for rushes, which make poor animal fodder. Burning briefly and brightly, rushlights made in rural Britain from the fat-soaked, dried pith of rush stems were familiar lights until the end of the nineteenth century. In his discourse on the

English longhorn cattle grazing grasses in a rush-dominated meadow in central Oxford.

economics of rushlight manufacture, clergyman Gilbert White, the eighteenth-century chronicler of the natural history of Selborne, took particular care to recommend the use of soft rush – one of the continuous-pithed rushes.[2] Soft rush is also widely used in basketry and mat-making, while mown rushes were familiar floor coverings in medieval Europe.[3] However, despite the belief of Rubens and many subsequent artists, biblical bulrushes are neither true rushes nor reed mace; they are sedges. Indeed, biblical bulrushes are probably the most famous of all sedges – they were used in papyrus, which was the basis of Dynastic Egyptian administration and record keeping.

Sedges

Sedges belong to a large, cosmopolitan family of some 4,500 species in over 90 genera, although more than 50 per cent of the species are found in only two genera, *Carex* and *Cyperus*. The Cyperaceae is the third most speciose monocotyledon family after the orchids and grasses, and may dominate some areas, for example bogs, in temperate regions and on tropical mountains. In Canada approximately 10 per cent of all flowering plants are sedges.[4] Research on British plants has been conducted for over half a millennium. They are therefore very well known compared with plants in most other parts of the world. Yet new discoveries are still sometimes made; in 1923, for example, Lady Joanna Davy and Gertrude Bacon discovered bristle sedge growing on a Scottish mountainside.[5] Despite its insignificant appearance, bristle sedge, scarcely more than 15 centimetres tall, has a vast bipolar distribution, extending from the North Pole through the Andes to the extreme southern tip of South America.[6] Deer grasses, with their diminutive drumstick-like flowering heads, and cotton grasses, with their rabbit-tailed fruiting heads, are familiar sedges of north-temperate wetlands. The umbrella-like inflorescences of papyrus and its relatives are memorable features of these riverine plants and field weeds in the tropics and subtropics. The sprawling, razor-sharp stems of tropical sclerias, clambering over forest and riverside plants, are a constant irritation to the unwary. Sedge flowers appear superficially similar to those of grasses, and traditionally have been used as evidence that sedges and grasses are closely related. However, DNA analysis of sedges suggests that they are more closely related to rushes than to grasses.

Humans make use of few sedge species, either directly or indirectly. In ancient Egypt papyrus was manufactured from papyrus sedge growing on the banks of the River Nile. In the making of papyrus, the stem of the plant is stripped of its outer layers and the inner pith is cut into long, thick strips. The strips are laid side by side, and a second layer of strips is laid at right angles to the first. The layered strips are soaked in water before they are hammered together to produce a single sheet of papyrus. The hammered sheet is crushed to extract the water, and the dried sheet is polished to produce a high-quality writing surface.[7] Papyrus sheets are fragile and cannot be folded, which is why long papyrus documents were produced as scrolls.

Thousands of examples of papyri (documents written on papyrus) have been found and provide glimpses into the lives of ancient

opposite: Inflorescence of the papyrus sedge unfolding.

peoples from the Mediterranean and Near East. Not only do papyri catalogue people's daily lives; by using carbon-dating techniques it is also possible to determine when the plant used to make a particular piece of papyrus was growing and hence the age of a piece of text.[8]

Papyrus stems were used in many other aspects of Egyptian life, such as basket-making and boat construction. In 1969 the adventurer Thor

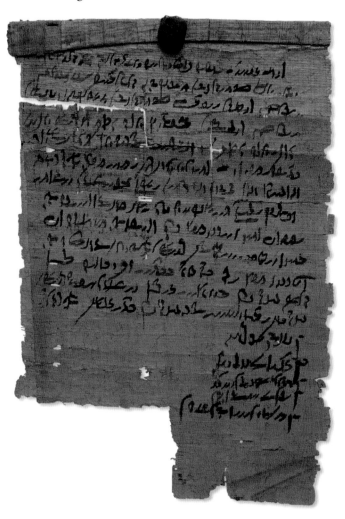

Ptolemeic (c. 194 BCE) legal document written on papyrus, describing the loan of wheat and barley, and illustrating how papyrus was constructed from two separate layers of stem strips.

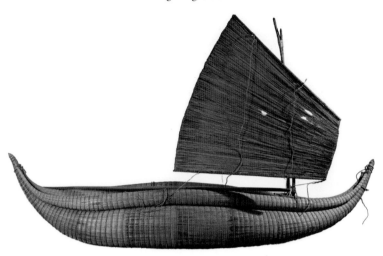

Boat, made from totora sedge, from Lake Titicaca, Bolivia.

Heyerdahl attempted to cross the Atlantic from Morocco in the boat *Ra*, made from bundles of papyrus stems and modelled on an Ancient Egyptian craft, to show that it was possible for mariners of the ancient Old World to cross the Atlantic Ocean. He succeeded the following year in *Ra II*, made from bundles of the New World sedge totora, widely used for boat construction around Lake Titicaca, Peru, but rather different from papyrus.[9] For thousands of years, across Asia and North Africa, the sedge, sweet galingale, has been used for scent, while Herodotus reports that Scythian kings were embalmed with oil extracted from sedge tubers, probably nutgrass.[10]

The Value of Distinction

One might ask whether nice distinctions among grasses, rushes and sedges are important outside the narrow confines of academia.[11] Few grasses, sedges or rushes are toxic; misidentifications are unlikely to have serious health effects on humans or their livestock. However, confused taxonomy may have immediate economic consequences. In the eighteenth and nineteenth centuries, the Falkland Islands were of immense value to the British as a restocking point for crews rounding

Cape Horn as they sailed between Europe and East Asia across the Pacific. Vast numbers of cattle had been introduced to the islands, and explorers of the southern oceans were impressed by tussac-grass, which was 'like a thick-set copsewood', with leaves nearly 2 metres long and edible, hazelnut-flavoured roots. Travellers returned to Europe with tales of the ease with which tussac-grass grew in extreme conditions to produce a highly nutritious fodder.[12] For the 'proprietors of unprofitable sandy and peaty soils throughout the British Dominions',[13] tussac-grass brought the dream that the unprofitable might be made profitable. Consequently, there was enormous interest in procuring plants and seed of this 'miracle grass'. Unfortunately, the first attempts to secure detailed descriptions of the grass met with disappointment when it was confused with the far less useful tussock sedge. The mistake was soon spotted, but opportunities for collecting a potentially important economic grass in an outpost of the empire were lost while the error was corrected.

Ecologically, habitats dominated by sedges and rushes usually indicate heavy or acidic soils in poorly drained land. Such areas have marginal use for grazing and are difficult to convert to fields without investment in drainage, deep ploughing using heavy animals or tractors, and the input of large amounts of fertilizer.[14] Such factors significantly decrease the economic returns likely from a plot of land dominated by sedges and rushes, compared with the returns from a similar plot dominated by grasses. Sedges and rushes are generally much less nutritious than grasses unless conditions are particularly poor. Furthermore, sedges and rushes do not recover from the depredations of grazers as rapidly as do grasses. It is primarily due to their nutritional value, whether as human food or animal fodder, that grasses have become so important to people.

four

Civilizing Humans

Unless your hoe is ever ready to assail the weeds, your voice to terrify the birds, your knife to check the shade over the darkened land, and your prayers to invoke the rain, . . . you will be shaking oaks in the woods to assuage your hunger.

VIRGIL, *Georgics*

Approximately 16,000 years ago the ice sheet that had encased much of the northern hemisphere for ten millennia began to melt. Plants and animals had been exterminated, driven to warmer climates or forced to adapt to the changed conditions. In Europe pockets of plant and animal diversity formed on the fringes of the Mediterranean, while further north areas not covered with ice resembled tundra grasslands. Once the thaw began, the animals and plants that were adapted to cold conditions either died, retreated north or withdrew to higher altitudes. Like Moses crossing the Sinai Desert, the thaw was slow, uneven and inconstant; it took 6,000 years. There was plenty of time for organisms to adapt to the new habitats; evolutionary opportunities were there to be exploited. When water is locked away in ice, sea levels are reduced and land bridges between continents are exposed. As glaciers oscillated land bridges appeared and disappeared, periodically isolating plant and animal populations. The biological consequences of these global events are stamped into the DNA of today's plants and animals.

Ten thousand years ago the thaw was complete. The hunter-gatherer subsistence of humans during the Ice Age gradually gave way to agrarian lifestyles. Humans were embarking on the most dramatic innovation in their evolutionary history since hominids had migrated out of Africa some 60 millennia earlier. Grasses were at the very heart of this innovation, in that they fed the expanding human population. Different grasses were cultivated in different regions: wheat and barley in the Near East, maize in Mexico, mango in the Chilean Andes, African rice, sorghum and pearl millet in West and sub-Saharan Africa, finger millet and tef in Ethiopia, Asian rice and Job's tears in central China, common millet and foxtail millet in northern China, barnyard millet in Japan and sugar cane in Papua New Guinea. Humans were starting to control the lives of grasses, and grasses were starting to control the lives of humans; Virgil caught the dichotomy succinctly when he wrote about Roman wheat farming.

Wheat Biology and Origins

Wheat, the staff of life, is the second most important food grass to humans. The wheat grain, packed with starchy endosperm and high levels of protein, provides a concentrated, compact source of calories, which enabled societies as diverse as those of Sumeria, Egypt, Greece and Rome to develop and transform the physical and intellectual ancient world. Arguably, wheat is the foundation of Western civilization, philosophy, religion and science. Understanding its origin has been a major biological challenge since the emergence of modern science in fifteenth-century Europe.

Wheat belongs to a small genus of annual grasses distributed from the Mediterranean to China, and is closely related to other grasses, including ephemeral goat grasses.[1] Importantly for hunter-gatherers, wild wheat and goat grasses grow en masse, are readily harvested and produce grains annually. Consequently, such grasses provided predictable food supplies as nomadic or semi-nomadic peoples moved

opposite: Winter bread wheat.

from place to place. One area where wheats and their close relatives are concentrated is the Fertile Crescent, the cradle of Western agriculture, which extends in a long arc through biblical lands, from the Red Sea north along the eastern Mediterranean into northern Syria, before sweeping east through southern Turkey, then southeast along the Iraq–Iran border. The presence of fragments of wheat and barley grains in archaeological sites implies that farming emerged among sedentary hunter-gatherer communities in the western arm of the Fertile Crescent.

The unifying principle of modern biology is Darwinian evolution: a rational process invoked to explain plant and animal diversity. The vista Charles Darwin and the Augustinian monk Gregor Mendel, the father of modern genetics, opened to understanding the diversity of life on Earth is based on variation in natural populations, the inheritance of genetic information from one generation to the next and the selection of genetic types, through time, that are adapted to particular environments. All plants and animals, including humans, are governed by evolutionary processes, despite humans having spent 10,000 years trying to separate themselves from these processes.

The wheat with which we are familiar is the product of astonishing natural genetic modifications. The basic outline of wheat's origin has been known for more than a century. The details of the puzzle have been gradually filled in as tools for tracing the events involved have become more sophisticated. However, the picture remains incomplete. One can take the analogy of trying to understand how a computer works. Rummaging around in the back may give you some ideas, and jabbing a screwdriver among the circuit boards will provide basic mechanistic information. However, a complete understanding of the computer involves careful dissection of all the various components. Since the detailed dissection of wheat and other grasses has come from developments in genetics, it is necessary to make a diversion into basic genetics.

Plant genes are strung along the double-helix of DNA molecules, wound into discrete structures called chromosomes. The nucleus of every cell, except pollen and eggs, of a typical grass contains two sets of chromosomes (that is, two genomes); such plants are described as diploid. For example, cultivated barley contains fourteen chromosomes; seven chromosomes in each genome. If each genome is given a letter, the genomic constitution of cultivated barley can be summarized as VV.

In a diploid grass each gene can exist in two forms. The form of the gene that is expressed is described as dominant over the other, recessive form. If the two forms are the same, the individual is homozygous (either dominant or recessive) for that gene; if the two forms are different the individual is heterozygous. Consider a gene that usually produces red glumes but occasionally, because of a rare mutation, produces yellow glumes. If there are two copies of the red form of the gene (that is, a red homozygote) then the plant will have red glumes; if there are two copies of the yellow form of the gene (that is, a yellow homozygote) then the glumes will be yellow. However, if there is one red form and one yellow form of the gene (that is, a red heterozygote) the glumes will be red. The genetic constitution of a grass is its genotype; the expression of that genotype, in a particular environment, is its phenotype. Furthermore, genetic outcomes of crosses between different genotypes are predictable. Crossing red homozygotes with yellow homozygotes will produce only red heterozygote offspring. Crossing red homozygotes with red heterozygotes will produce, on average, 50 per cent red heterozygote offspring and 50 per cent red homozygote offspring. Crossing red heterozygotes with each other will produce, on average, 25 per cent red homozygote, 50 per cent red heterozygote and 25 per cent yellow homozygote offspring.

Grasses with more than two chromosome sets are called polyploids. For example, grasses with four chromosome sets are tetraploids, and those with six sets are hexaploids. Polyploids with odd numbers of chromosome sets, for example those with three sets (triploids), tend to be sterile. Generally, polyploids have more than two forms of each gene, and tend to be larger, more productive, more variable and evolutionarily fitter than diploids. Many cultivated grasses are polyploids.

Between half a million and three million years ago, a diploid wild wheat (AA; *Triticum urartu*) and a diploid goat grass (BB; *Aegilops speltoides*) hybridized to produce tetraploid wild emmer (AABB), which combined the genomes of the two species. Wild emmer was a successful evolutionary experiment. It spread from its region, or regions, of origin throughout much of the Near East long before it was used by humans. In the Jordan Valley and Syria, 23,000 years ago, wild emmer grew alongside einkorn, another wild diploid wheat, and was being used by early hunter-gatherers. Ten to twelve millennia ago, the domestication of wild emmer and einkorn began.

Cultivated emmer, together with barley, became the staples of civilizations that stretched from Egypt through Mesopotamia to the Indus Valley, and was only superseded, by another evolutionary experiment in wheat genetics, about 2,000 years ago. In cultivated emmer, harvested grains are surrounded by tough glumes that make the grains difficult to clean. In contrast, another type of domesticated emmer, called durum wheat, has glumes that are readily lost. It is durum wheat that is used to make pasta in all of its multifarious forms.

Ancient Egyptian wheat grains.

The new experiment was the origin of modern hexaploid bread wheat (AABBDD). Some seven to ten millennia ago in Transcaucasia, hybridization between cultivated emmer and another goat grass (DD; *Aegilops tauschii*) produced modern bread wheat. This hybridization event appears to have occurred at different times and in different places, producing slightly different genetic outcomes.[2] One of these we call spelt, which is still cultivated in parts of the Mediterranean. For much of its history bread wheat has had social cachet. It can be used to make light, easily digested bread but since the species' geographic range was limited it was expensive; the rich flaunted it, the poor desired it and monarchs lost their heads over it.

Humans Alter Wheat

The apparently simple act of picking a grain of wild wheat, saving it and planting it had profound consequences for both plant and humans; this was the beginning of wheat domestication. Generations of hunter-gatherers collected the wild wheats around them for food without changing the plants substantially. However, between 11,500 and 13,000 years ago, hunter-gatherers started to plant the gathered seed. Archaeological evidence shows that this change in behaviour is correlated with the climate getting warmer and drier, and large mammals being hunted to the verge of extinction. To be successfully domesticated, grasses not only had to be good food sources but had to have the right genetics. That is, the characters that made plants easy to cultivate and manage were under simple genetic control and easily selected, albeit unconsciously. Numerous adaptations make up the so-called 'domestication syndrome' that separates wild from cultivated wheats. Compared with wild cereals, the adaptations shown by primitive domesticates make harvesting easier, enhance seedling competition and increase seed production. Not only are these adaptations of great biological and economic interest, but they are also invaluable archaeological markers to understanding the remnants of cultures across numerous sites, distributed from Western Europe through the Mediterranean, North Africa and the Levant, to Central Asia and northern India.

The most conspicuous feature associated with harvesting is the non-shattering trait of cultivated wheats. Wild cereals drop their grains at maturity; the stalk holding the spikelet breaks, and the grain is dispersed and eventually germinates to form the next generation. This feature is controlled by two genes in wheat; as a result of mutations grains are either not shed or only partially shed. Under natural conditions the non-shattering mutation is at a disadvantage. However, if grains are harvested, non-shattering ones will be preferentially collected, whilst the shattering ones will escape the harvester. If the harvest is planted, the cereal that emerges will contain more individuals with non-shattering grains than individuals with shattering grains. Over numerous generations all cultivated plants will become non-shattering. Experiments with einkorn have shown that non-shattering plants can be selected from shattering plants in 20 to 100 years. The archaeological evidence indicates that this trans - formation was much slower; in wheat it took 1,500 years and in barley 2,000 years.[3] Curiously, in areas where grains are harvested by beating mature plants, rather than cutting them down, the non-shattering trait has no selective advantage and is not part of the 'domestication syndrome'.

Another important element of the 'domestication syndrome' is associated with seedling competition. Grains that contribute to the seed bank and germinate at different times, as happens in wild wheats, are means of spreading risk. If a proportion of the grains germinate but are then killed by the weather, other grains can germinate and contribute to the next generation. A wheat field, even a very primitive field, is a very different environment from the wild habitat. By scratching the land with a primitive plough, a seedbed is created and competition among species is reduced by weeding, but competition between cereal seedlings is intense. Those grains that germinate first or produce the biggest seedlings produce the plants that are harvested for the next generation. Cultivated wheats have large,

Pieter Bruegel the Elder's *The Harvesters* (1565) showing shoulder-high cereals.

uniform, short, fat grains; wild wheats have small, variable, long, thin grains. Furthermore, the grains of wild wheats are described as hulled; the glumes, lemmas and paleas (chaff) are firmly attached to the grain. Chaff modifies grain dormancy. The grains of cultivated wheats are not surrounded by tough, persistent, protective chaff; they are described as naked. Hunter-gatherers collected cereal spikelets; early farmers collected naked grains. The distinction is another clue used by archaeologists interested in understanding local economies.

Wheat Alters Humans

The expression sorting the wheat from the chaff – separating the valued from the valueless – has its origins in the harvest, but as a metaphor it fails to recognize that chaff (glumes, lemmas and paleas) once protected the grain during its early development; the exceptional require the unexceptional to succeed. Thus, if we want to know about people's lives we must focus on the graves, rubbish heaps and middens of common people. Human skeletons tell us about the quality of people's diets, and something about how they lived and died; they also allow us to estimate the sizes of their populations. The leavings of everyday life tell us what people lived on and what lived on them. As we have seen, grasses are important for the health and wealth of civilizations; they also change human populations – socially, economically, politically and genetically.

Grass-based agriculture increased the quantity and predictability of the food supply, but not necessarily its quality. Compared with the diets of their hunter-gatherer ancestors, early agriculturalists' diets were low in proteins and vitamins but high in carbohydrates. Humans had spent generations genetically adapting to hunter-gatherer lifestyles, so were, initially, probably poorly adapted to life as sedentary farmers.

Cereal grains, including wheat, are not just packets of benign carbohydrate and proteins; they also contain compounds that might be detrimental to health. Cereal grains have high levels of phytates, chemicals that interfere with mineral absorption by our guts. One of these minerals is iron, an element essential for the function of red blood cells. Consequently, skeletons of millennia of people raised on cereal-rich diets, from across the globe, show symptoms of iron deficiency; the more intensive the agriculture, the more pronounced

Group of Egyptian wooden figures (c. 2050–2000 BC) showing the processes involved in brewing: the figures at the back are using querns to grind grains.

the symptoms.[4] In addition to the phytate problem, early wheat domestication inadvertently selected forms with very low levels of iron in the milled grains. The archaeological record also shows that people in agricultural societies suffered from calcium and vitamin D deficiencies.[5] People had become more susceptible to disease; they lived longer but were sicker than their hunter-gatherer ancestors. As they started living cheek by jowl, there were ample opportunities for the rapid spread of diseases.

In early agricultural communities, a dramatic decline in the health of individuals is correlated with the adoption of this lifestyle. For the vast majority of human history, our lives have been 'nasty, brutish and short'. Individuals over 50 years old were considered venerable; they had survived the rigours of childhood, the risks of fatal injury and the lottery of infectious disease. The lives of hunter-gatherer women were shorter than those of men; they had to endure the gamble of child-birth and the stresses of child rearing. However, in the eastern Mediterranean, following the adoption of agriculture, the lifespan of women increased, despite the poorer diet; life appears to have become a little less risky for women.

Cereals are easier to chew than wild-collected plant foods. Acceptance of the agricultural life led to changes in the human face and teeth; jaws have become more delicate and teeth smaller in the last 10,000 years.[6] More dramatic still was the effect of cereal farming on the heights of adults. In the Near East, coincident with the spread of extensive agriculture (*c.* 11,000 years ago), there was a steady decline in adult height until about 4,000 years ago. The heights of adult agriculturalists fell by 16 centimetres for men and 13 centimetres for women compared with those of hunter-gatherers. Despite a gradual increase in average human height over the last four millennia, we are still about 3 centimetres shorter than our hunter-gatherer ancestors.[7] Similar effects are found across cultures in Eurasia and the Americas that adopted grass-based diets. Poor diet led to poor growth of people. Environment (poor food quality) combined with human genotypes to produce short people. Those individuals lucky enough to carry the right genes, and escape factors such as disease and accident, survived to breed, ensuring that their offspring had a greater chance of survival than their less fit peers; evolution in action.

The low vitamin content of cereal grains had dramatic effects on northern Europeans, thousands of kilometres away from the areas of wheat domestication. Without adequate vitamin D, humans develop rickets. If the vitamin cannot be obtained from food it must be synthesized in the skin from sunlight. Once African hominids had lost their body hair they soon developed a deeply pigmented skin to protect them from harmful ultraviolet radiation. Vitamin D synthesis was therefore reduced, but this was not a problem at tropical latitudes. However, as hominids migrated out of Africa, into less sunny areas, rickets become prevalent. Northern populations adapted in two ways. Skin tones became lighter, so more sunlight could be used to synthesize vitamin D, but at the risk of increased skin cancer.[8] Like most mammals, adult humans are lactose intolerant, that is, they cannot digest lactose, the main sugar of milk. However, fair-skinned adult northern Europeans started to consume milk, a good source of vitamin D and calcium; they were lactose tolerant. The lactose-tolerance mutation appears to have originated about 8,000 years ago and spread rapidly though northern Europeans.[9] Oetzi, the 5,300-year-old Iceman whose corpse was discovered in a glacier in the Italian Alps in 1991, was lactose intolerant.[10] Lactose tolerance is also found in East African pastoralists, and is caused by a different mutation from that found in northern populations.[11] The rapid spread of the mutation indicates that it was highly advantageous. Mutations in genes associated with insulin regulation and alcohol breakdown are also associated with carbohydrate-dominated cereal diets.

Grasses changed us; we carry the evidence of the slow genetic adaptations to the agricultural lifestyle and our reliance on cereals in our genes.

Wheat Alters Societies

The social, cultural and political changes of sedentary civilizations are preserved in the archaeological record. Complex material cultures developed; possessions no longer needed to be portable. Food could be stored for long periods and seeds preserved between growing seasons; wealth could accumulate. Societies became stratified and governments surfaced; elites emerged.

The old adage runs that money does not grow on trees. However, the means to weigh precious metals accurately, and all that follows for economic development in civilized societies, can be found growing on grasses. In Ancient Greece a drachma contained 18 *kerata* (or carets); each *keras* was equivalent to four wheat grains. The Irish Celts used eight wheat grains to one *pingin*, and for more than 600 years, from Alfred the Great to the start of the Tudor Dynasty, the English fixed the weight of a penny as 32 grains of wheat. Besides Graeco-Roman civilizations, the Assyrians (and all the measurement systems of the Near East), Persians, Hindus and Arabs used wheat grains as their basic measurement units. If only barley was available, all these systems had an 'exchange rate' of approximately three barley grains to four wheat grains. In Sumatra and Madagascar rice grains were used to define the smallest units of weight. The classicist and expert on historical measurement standards, William Ridgeway, used differences in the

Roman silver denarius coin with wheat ears around the margin.

distribution of wheat and rice to infer that the Hindu weight system must have originated in northern India since wheat, rather than rice, was the standard.[12]

Using cereal grains as weight and currency standards implies considerable uniformity across individual grains. The framers of English laws under Edward I and Henry VII were aware that grain sizes varied across wheat ears and tried to close such loopholes; 'the penny sterling should weigh 32 grains of wheat, round and dry, and taken from the midst of the ear', and 'every sterling to be of the weight of thirty-two grains of wheat that grew in the midst of the ear of wheat', respectively. Arguments abound as to whether cereal grains were ever really used as practical weights and measures. Whatever the case, cereals were evidently important enough, in multiple cultures, to be associated with rigorous weights and measures systems, whether literal or metaphorical. In the nineteenth century the French artist Louis-Oscar Roty made *The Sower*, which is a familiar image on French stamps. However, Roty had little appreciation of agricultural practice; the seed is being broadcast into the wind, where it would be blown back towards the sower rather than across the field.

Besides being used in weights and measures, cereal grains play a role in the legendary origins of chess, and the mathematics of large numbers. The main characters, a parsimonious ruler and a shrewd but naive inventor, whether in India or China, are common; the epoch and culture change. The potentate offers the inventor a reward for inventing chess. The inventor asks that a single grain of cereal be placed on the first square of the board, two grains on the second square, four on the third and so on, until all 64 of the board's squares are filled. The ruler agreed to what seems like a miniscule reward, a few grains of cereal; the inventor knows otherwise. It is impossible for the ruler to fulfil the promise. Indeed, so vast is the number of grains required to fill the board that the total global production of rice, wheat or barley in the last 10,000 years could not meet the reward.[13]

Due to the complexities of wheat genetics and the ease with which wheats and their wild relatives hybridize and double their chromosome numbers, there is plenty of variation upon which natural and artificial selection can operate. The palette of wheat genetics was being filled, and humans could start to mix colours to produce the wheat plants best suited for their purposes. At first mixing was blind, driven by luck more than judgement, but as more become known the mixing became more objective. The vision of many, and the nightmare of some, is that humans will start making their own colours, rather than relying on natural colours, to create the wheats (and other cereal crops) needed for the future. However, the ready availability of cereal-based food came at a cost. We had to adapt to our new food supply, and accept that cultivating grasses cannot happen without the destruction of the natural world.

five

Confusing Botanists

Near the leaves it [Job's tears] grows . . . little stones, white and round as pearls, as big as a chick-pea but as hard as a stone. . . . I have never seen anything among plants that filled me with greater wonder. So charming the adornment that one might think that the jeweller's art had arranged gleaming white pearls symmetrically among the leaves; so elegantly solved is the problem of causing a gem to grow from a plant!

PLINY, *Natural History*

Christopher Columbus's rediscovery of the New World in the late fifteenth century had profound effects on the intellectual perceptions and lives of Western Europeans and the biology of the planet. It shattered ecclesiastical certainties and the faith of intellectuals in the veracity of Greco-Roman authorities, established anthropogenic biological interchange across the Atlantic Ocean and changed food cultures. As people began to break away from dogmatic beliefs that plants were God given and could not change, they started to wonder from whence different plants came, especially those plants upon which they most relied. Such speculations were not just academic exercises for natural historians; they concerned how human cultures and civilizations developed and ultimately provided raw material for the Darwinian ideas that would come to dominate biology and other disciplines during the twentieth century. Europeans were familiar with startling plants and animals from the east, including grasses such as Job's tears and bamboos. Such 'natural productions', real, imagined and forged, were cherished features of cabinets of curiosities; the Americas offered even more curios for the curious.[1]

The first explorers of the New World were fortune hunters, warriors, priests and administrators with few sympathies for the native inhabitants or their ways of life. At the end of his life, as he reflected on the fate of his colleagues, the conquistador Bernal Díaz del Castillo was frank about their motives: 'they died in the service of God and his majesty, and to give light to those who sat in darkness, – *and also to acquire that wealth which most men covet*'.[2] The wealth to which Díaz referred was gold and silver, not the many remarkable New World plants, of which one of the most unusual, and useful, was maize. Wherever Europeans went they found that maize had entered into all aspects of Amerindian life, from food and medicine to ritual and worship. Gonzalo Fernández de Oviedo y Valdés's *De La Natural Hystoria de Las Indias* ('Of the Natural History of the Indies', 1526), the first attempt to produce a comprehensive account of the natural history of the Americas, described the maize agriculture he witnessed

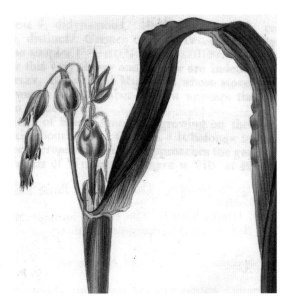

Detail from William Curtis's illustration of Job's tears, 1824.

in present-day Costa Rica, together with the milling of the grain and the preparation of maize bread. Europeans with experience of the Americas came to appreciate maize as a food, at least compared with other foodstuffs. However, at least one country-bound, sixteenth-century Englishman had a rather different opinion:

> Turky wheate [maize] doth nourish far less than either Wheate, Ric, Barly or Otes. The bread which is made there-of if meanly white . . . it is hard and drie as bisket is . . . it is of hard digestion, and yeeldeth to the body little nourish-ment, it slowly descendeth and bindeth the belly . . . the barbarous Indians which know no better, are constrained to make a virtue of necessitie, and think it good food . . . a more conuenient foode for swine than for men.[3]

Maize

The English botanist Henry Lyte, in his 1578 English translation of Rembert Dodoens's *Cruydeboeck*, considered maize, 'a marveilous strange plante, nothing resembling any other kind of grayne'.[4] In its vegetative state maize, or corn,[5] appears similar to other tall, annual grasses. However, when maize produces flowers and fruit, some four months after planting, it looks very different. The main stem has a terminal tassel of male flowers, which Lyte, having no understanding of floral and pollen function, described as 'idle and barren eares, which bring foorth nothing but the flowers'. Pressed close to the main stem there are large cobs of tightly packed female flowers surrounded by leaf-like husks and topped by a mass of silky styles. Each female flower, with its long, thin style, produces a single maize kernel or, in Lyte's words, 'bringeth foorth his seede'.

A maize kernel, about the 'bigness of a pease',[6] is similar in structure to any other grass fruit, comprising an embryo and starch-packed endosperm, together with seed and fruit walls. There are two sorts of endosperm, hard and soft, which define the main maize types. 'Dents'

The first image of maize was published in Leonard Fuchs's *De historia stirpium commentarii insignes* (1542).

TVRCICVM
FRVMENTVM.
Türckisch korn,
New England whont.

have a hard and soft endosperm, so as the kernel matures the soft endosperm contracts to produce a depression in the top of the kernel. In 'flints' and 'popcorns' the endosperm is hard, but in the latter the endosperm expands and the kernel bursts when it is heated. In 'floury' sorts the endosperm is soft, whilst in the 'sweet corns' the endosperm is sucrose rich. Globally grown modern maize cultivars usually produce one or two large yellow cobs per plant, each cob having a thick, tough centre surrounded by rows of kernels. In contrast, traditional Latin American maize cobs are tremendously diverse in kernel colours, ranging from white through yellow and red, to brown

Part of the colour variation found in the cobs of traditionally grown maize landraces in Latin America.

and black, and in the sizes and numbers of cobs per plant. Less than a century after the discovery of the New World, Lyte described maize growing in Europe with 'sometimes browne, sometimes red, and sometimes white' kernels.[7] The herbalist John Gerard uses highly descriptive names for the maize plants he knew: 'white Turkie Wheate', 'Yellow Turkie Wheate', 'Golden coloured Turkie Wheate', 'Red Turkie Wheate' and 'Blew and white Turkie Wheate'.[8]

Botanically, maize belongs to the genus *Zea*, a small group of usually annual Mexican and Central American grasses that also includes wild grasses known as teosintes. *Zea* is closely related to perennial *Tripsacum*, or the gama grasses, a small genus of grasses distributed from the southern United States to Paraguay.

Discovering Origins

Domestication is a dynamic biological process where heritable genetic changes happen in a group of plants because of their interactions with humans; eventually the plants become dependent on humans for their survival. The discovery of origins is complicated since crops evolve and adapt as humans move them away from the places where they were first domesticated. Furthermore, different academic disciplines must collaborate to integrate evidence from sources as diverse as morphology, biogeography, history, philology, archaeology, carbon dating, genetics, phylogeny and developmental biology; individual researchers into crop origins can rapidly find themselves outside their intellectual comfort zones.

In the mid-nineteenth century the French-Swiss botanist Alphonse de Candolle was hampered in his investigations of crop origins by the limited range of plant fragments recovered from archaeological sites, the difficulties of producing reliable dates for objects based on archaeological context alone and the difficulties of objectively determining plant relationships. In the early twentieth century the Soviet geneticist Nikolai Vavilov focused his investigations of crop origins on collecting samples grown in areas of high crop diversity, and where species similar to cultivated plants were found. He reasoned that local cultivars (called landraces) would be highly adapted to the places in which they grew and the conditions under which they were managed. Hence they would contain a reservoir of genes, some of which would be similar to those of the wild relatives.

Developments in archaeology, physics, philosophy of science, computing and genetics have removed many impediments for modern investigators of crop origins. As a result of refinements in archaeological field techniques, leaf fragments, small seeds, pollen grains and phytoliths are readily recovered from sites. Following the development and refinement of carbon-dating technologies, miniscule samples of individual plant fragments can be dated. Because of the development of rigorous methods for reconstructing species

Specimen of maize collected in Europe in the early 18th century, with immature female cob and male tassel.

relationships, and accessing cheap, powerful computers, phylogenies are readily built. Furthermore, due to the ability to sequence any DNA fragment, vast amounts of genetic data are readily available. Yet, since the end of the Second World War, changes in global agricultural practice have resulted in local crop diversity being eradicated at an alarming rate.

Two arguments have dogged discussions of maize origins. The first concerns the question of whether maize occurred in the Old World before the discovery of the New World. The second relates to the consideration of whether maize originated directly from a single wild species (teosinte hypothesis) or multiple species (tripartite hypothesis).

New World or Old World?

In the 1960s the American cultural geographer Carl Sauer argued that maize was found in the Old World before Columbus.[9] The evidence he used came from interpreting names and descriptions in manuscripts and early printed sources. However, since no botanical specimens survive to verify reports, linking and verifying names across languages, cultures and time is fraught with pitfalls. In 1837, using bibliographic evidence, de Candolle was uncompromising in his view that maize was American, not European or Asian, although the French agronomist Matthieu Bonafous argued for pre-Columbian maize in the Old World, and the American geologist Peter Browne blustered that until he personally intervened the debate was unresolved.[10]

Both sides of the debate agreed that maize was unknown in ancient Greek and Roman literature. However, reference to seeds, interpreted as maize kernels, in two pre-1492 documents from Italy and Persia, and a grass illustration in a Chinese text from the late sixteenth century, were used as the basis for the theory of an eastern origin of maize.[11] The Italian manuscript was shown to be a forgery, whilst the grasses depicted in the Persian and Chinese documents were shown to be millet or sorghum. In November 1493 the Italian cleric and scholar Pietro Martyr d'Anghiera wrote to his patron Cardinal Ascanio Sforza and described a cereal he called maize. Besides including the first recorded use of the word maize, Martyr's statement has been used as evidence that maize was known in the Old World before Columbus presented his New World booty to the Spanish Court in May 1493.[12] The evidence relies on Martyr's assertion that the cereal presented by Columbus was identical to a cereal being grown around Grenada and Milan, but Martyr appears to have confused maize with the cereal sorghum. Forty-three years after Columbus, the French botanist and physician Jean Ruel made the first printed mention of *Frumentum Turcicum* (Turkish corn), noting that 'in the days of our grandfathers' it came from Greece or Asia.[13] However, European local names, such as Roman corn (used in Lorraine), Barbary corn (Provence), Sicilian corn (Tuscany) and Egyptian corn (Turkey), emphasized where people believed maize came from rather than where it originated. Thus, an eastern origin for maize cannot be inferred from popular names in circulation during the sixteenth century, such as Turkish wheat or corn, Indian corn, *blé de Turquie*, *Frumentum Turcicum* or *Frumentum Asiaticum Indicum*.

The *Vinland Sagas* report 'fields of self-sown wheat',[14] and an abundance of grapes, in an area that is today thought to be New Brunswick, Canada. The *Sagas*, written down in the early thirteenth century, recount Leif Erikson's discovery of the New World some five centuries before Columbus's arrival. In 1885 an American agronomist equated Erikson's 'wheat' with maize,[15] throwing historians of crop plants into confusion and opening up the possibility that maize was grown in the Old World before Columbus rediscovered the New World. However, Erikson is most unlikely to have seen maize so far north, and since maize is so distinctive, he would surely not have compared it to wheat.

Furthermore, there are no unambiguous reports of maize from ancient Old World cultures such as Egypt and China; no maize cobs or kernels have ever been recovered from Old World archaeological sites and there are no close relatives of maize in the Old World.

Mexican doll showing one of the many non-food uses to which maize leaves and cob husks are put.

Overall, the picture is clear; maize is one of a handful of crops, including tomatoes, potatoes and chillies, whose widespread Old World distribution occurred after 1492.

Following its introduction to Iberia, maize was recorded from France, Iraq, southern India, Thailand and Japan in the sixteenth century. During the seventeenth century it expanded through Southeast Asia, India and the northern Mediterranean, and made its first appearances in West Africa, South Africa and the Horn of Africa. The eighteenth century saw maize's expansion across Europe, and into the eastern Mediterranean, Egypt and China. In Africa maize gradually extended its range during the eighteenth century until by the end of the nineteenth century it was found across the entire continent. Maize took 400 years to cover the Old World; it had taken about 9,000 years to cover the New World.

One or Many Ancestors?

As European explorers island hopped through the Caribbean and marched across Central and South America they found maize culture well established. In Central America the pantheons of the Olmecs, Mayans, Aztecs and Toltecs were populated with deities,[16] who received ritual and sacrificial offerings of maize. The Toltecs and Aztecs believed that Quetzalcoatl, god of wisdom and knowledge, discovered maize and invented tortillas. The Aztecs also had separate male and female gods, Xochipilli and Chicomecoatl, for young maize plants, while Yum Kaax was the Mayan maize god. In 1555 the French Protestant minister Jean de Léry joined the attempt to establish a French Antarctic Colony in Brazil, around Rio de Janeiro. In *Histoire d'un voyage faict en la terre du Bresil, autrement dite Amerique* ('History of a Voyage to the Land of Brazil, also called America', 1578), along with lurid descriptions of cannibalism among the Tupinambá, who populated the region, he described the plants they used, one of which was maize. In 1620, as European crops failed around Massachusetts, the Pilgrim Fathers survived because the local Iroquois taught them to grow maize.

Maize has only ever been found associated with humans and their activities; it is not found in the wild. Furthermore, it looks very different from all other New World grasses, and consequently close wild relatives are not obvious. Given the prominence of maize in the lives of indigenous Americans, and the antiquity of its cultivation, determining maize ancestry cannot be resolved by rooting through libraries. Biological and archaeological fieldwork in the Americas is needed, combined with genetic and dating information. The answer to the question of origin is biologically important, and has profound implications for the interpretation of the New World archaeological record. This leads on to questions such as whether domestication occurred once or many times, and where and when this happened in the Americas.

The moist, warm Mesoamerican climate makes preservation of plant remains unlikely. The Near East is replete with sites suitable for crop preservation, but until recently most maize remains came from a handful of dry caves and rock shelters scattered in the southwestern United States and southern Mexico. These seasonally occupied sites contain layers of human refuse built up over thousands of years.

Mayan stone sculpture
(c. AD 715) from Copan
(Honduras) of a maize
god with a headdress
of a stylized cob and
hair in the form of
the silk.

By careful excavation, the layers can be peeled away and the plant and animal remnants retrieved, identified and dated. The ability to extract phytoliths, characteristic silica deposits inside grass cells, from archaeological soil samples, and analyse them for those types characteristic of domesticated maize, has increased the number and range of archaeological sites available for investigation in the last two decades.

In the caves of the Tehuacán Valley, along the watershed of the Rio de las Balsas, in southwestern Mexico, a chronological sequence of thousands of cobs and cob fragments has been discovered. Some of the oldest of these cobs are little more than 20 millimetres long, with eight rows of six to nine kernels. Significantly, each kernel is partially enclosed by a husk-like sheath. Furthermore, a modern maize race, Argentine pod corn, with cobs similar to those in the caves, was discovered growing in Argentina.

The tripartite hypothesis emerged from investigations of hybridization between maize and gama grasses. Under this theory, teosinte was a maize-gama grass hybrid. Maize itself was thought to have arisen from an extinct wild maize species with cobs similar to those of pod

Modern, highly bred maize cobs.

corn. The final element of the hypothesis was that domesticated maize in the Americas had been produced through repeated hybridization with teosinte.[17] However, close investigation of pod corn cobs showed that the kernels could not be dispersed naturally and needed humans; the cobs were not from wild plants, but from fully domesticated plants.[18] The role of hybridization as a botanical *deus ex machina* in the origin of maize was rejected.[19]

According to the teosinte hypothesis,[20] the sole maize progenitor is teosinte, a wild grass cultivated for food in which particular mutations were selected to improve the usefulness of teosinte. Flowerless teosinte, or 'grain of the gods', appears to be little more than a branched type of maize. However, when the kernels mature the differences become stark. Teosinte kernels are arranged in two-sided ears, with single kernels surrounded by hard shells that break apart at maturity. In contrast, maize kernels are arranged in multiple-sided cobs of soft, paired kernels, which remain attached to the cob at maturity. Maize cannot disperse its seeds naturally, but teosinte seeds are specialized for long-distance dispersal through animal guts. The hypothesis was originally proposed towards the end of the nineteenth century, but during the 1930s cytological and genetic data started to accumulate in support of it.

Extensive collecting of teosinte populations and maize cultivars across Mexico and Central America, followed by genetic investigations, revealed that one teosinte, *Zea mays* ssp. *parviglumis*, was more similar to domesticated maize than any other teosinte investigated. The wild relative of maize had been found. Furthermore, the change from teosinte to maize appears only to require the modification of three major genes. With modification of so few genes needed, it has been suggested that the teosinte-maize transformation may have happened in less than a decade.[21] Detailed examination of genetic variation across the geographical range of ssp. *parviglumis* showed that populations from the Rio de las Balsas were most similar to maize.[22] These data match with the earliest known maize fossils (*c.* 7,000 years old) from the Oaxacan Highlands.[23] However, the genetic data suggest that the original divergence between teosinte and domesticated maize may have happened up to 9,200 years ago.[24] Furthermore, all known maize cultivars can be traced to a single domestication event; if other domestication events occurred they have left no trace in the DNA of the multitude of maize types known today.

From the melting pot of domestication in southwestern Mexico, maize gradually spread through the Americas.[25] One route was into Guatemala, through the Caribbean and then South America, where maize was quickly established as a crop. The second route was through northern Mexico into the southwestern United States, then northeast to southern Canada, although maize culture was not fully established along this route until about 1,200 years ago.

Today, millions of hectares of maize, much of it genetically modi-fied, are grown worldwide, producing hundreds of millions of tonnes of kernels annually. Maize is a worldwide commodity, with traders speculating over maize futures. Most corn is used for the production of animal feed and, controversially, as a source of biofuels. Golden-yellow maize cobs and kernels crushed and toasted for cornflakes, exploded for popcorn and pulverized for polenta are familiar foods, while purified maize starch and syrup are frequent food additives across the globe. Maize, under guiding human hands, has moved a long way from the caves of the Tehuacán Valley.

six

Feeding Humans

☸

Peoples truly rich are those who cultivate cereals on a large scale.
. . . The least discovery in this field, whatever the political journals
may say, is more important for a country than a change of the party
in power. For it is the history of discoveries and inventions – in
the domain of nature, as well as in the intellectual field – that
constitutes the real history of civilizations.

ROBERT CHODAT, *Popular Science Monthly* (1913)

I n 1913 the Swiss botanist Robert Chodat thought that famine was
impossible in Europe; a year later nemesis arrived in the form of
the First World War. The war, together with the failure of harvests, natural disasters such as drought and floods, and political hubris
and incompetence, conspired to restrict European food supplies,
resulting in famine. Chodat believed that food grasses were the real
legacy of past generations, not the ephemeral baubles we manufacture
and with which we pack our museums. In 1941, as Germany turned
on the Soviet Union, one of Stalin's reactions to the threat of invasion was to order the Hermitage in Leningrad to be stripped of its
priceless artefacts as a precaution against them being pillaged. In
contrast, the priceless seed collections massed by the Bureau of
Applied Botany were all but ignored. Yet seeds, the products of generations of natural and artificial selection by peoples across the globe,
are as much cultural objects as the artworks that graced the rooms of
the Winter Palace.

By the 1930s, world-leading plant breeding institutes had been established in the Soviet Union and Germany. In 1935 Heinrich Himmler created a special Waffen SS research unit, the *Ahnenerbe*, to investigate cultural and anthropological history; given the long history of human-crop interactions it was natural that plants would come within this organization's remit. One recruit to the *Ahnenerbe* was Heinz Brücher, a young botanist who eventually became part of Himmler's personal staff. In 1943 Brücher led the SS Sammelkommando, charged with looting the seed stores, left behind by the Soviets in the Crimea and Ukraine, for German agriculture.[1] After the war Brücher escaped from Europe, established himself in South America and became a prominent advocate for the conservation of food-plant genetic resources before being killed in 1991.

Himmler's strategy was not unique; the history of crop breeding is littered with examples of seeds becoming valuable spoils of war or conquest to enhance the victor's food security. Dwarf wheat, one of the triumphs of modern plant breeding, was achieved by transferring 'reduced height' (Rht) genes from Japanese to Western wheats. The short wheat varieties originated as Korean landraces in the third and fourth centuries AD, and were transported to Japan in the sixteenth century during the Korean-Japanese War. Analyses of wheat DNA have shown that Rht genes spread around the world by three routes. The most important route was through the Japanese wheat variety 'Norin 10'; this originally arrived in the United States as a seed sample given to an American wheat breeder just after the Second World War. In the early 1950s 'Norin 10' started to be crossed with familiar North American wheats until, in the late 1960s, new dwarf wheat varieties were developed by the Nobel Peace Prize winner Norman Borlaug. These varieties were distributed globally and became the foundation of the 1970s Green Revolution. Other routes saw Rht genes being transferred to south and central European semi-dwarf winter wheats in the early twentieth century, and from Italy to Europe and the Soviet Union, via Argentina, after the Second World War.[2]

Population and Agriculture

Twelve thousand years ago, as grasses were first being domesticated in the Near East, there were three to four million people on Earth (about the population size of Brasília, Brazil). By the time Stonehenge was completed in *c.* 2000 BC the population had risen to about 27 million people. By the time of Christ the global human population was about 170 million (about the population of Nigeria), and at the start of the British agricultural revolution, in the late eighteenth century, it had risen to between 800 million and 1.1 billion. At the outbreak of the Second World War the world's population was about 2.2 billion, and on 31 October 2011 the human race officially reached 7 billion with the birth of Filipino Danica May Camacho.[3] By 2050 it is expected that there will be 9.1 billion people on the planet. However, human population increase over the last twelve millennia has not been inexorable. Crashes have occurred in the face of environmental change, for example the silting up and salting of the Sumerian rivers, the Tigris and Euphrates, and the erosion of Mediterranean hillsides *c.* 4,000 and *c.* 3,000 years ago, respectively.[4] Natural disasters, disease and political dogma have been persistent themes in the history of famines, for example the Indian famine of 1876–9, the Chinese famines of 1877–9, 1927 and 1959–61, and the Soviet famines of 1921–2 and 1932–3.

The total number of people on the planet is one indicator of total food needs, but the total weight of people is also important; heavier people need more calories just to keep going. It has been estimated that the weight of the global human population is 287 million tonnes, ranging from 12.2 Americans per tonne to 19.2 Eritreans per tonne. Ominously, the study's authors conclude that the fatter human population 'could have the same implications for world food energy demands as an extra half a billion people'.[5]

A little over a century before Chodat, Thomas Malthus, in *Principles of Population* (1798), argued that the human population grows faster than it is capable of producing adequate food. By the

Terracing is shown here creating tiny fields for planting wheat
and potatoes on the steep volcanic slopes of Tenerife.

mid-nineteenth century it was expected that population growth would
outstrip available food supply, but Malthus's prediction was wrong.
In 1968 ecologist Paul Ehrlich re-rehearsed Malthus's arguments
on population growth, and predicted widespread famine in the 1970s
and 1980s. Yet his predictions, like those of Malthus, were wrong.
Both underestimated the impact of agricultural research and the
Green Revolution on food production. The dividend of the Green
Revolution was a steady and dramatic rise in agricultural production;
global grain yields increased by 250 per cent between 1950 and
1984. However, this rise was underwritten by breeding genetically
uniform crops and loading the environment with industrial chemicals
such as fertilizers and pesticides, as prehistoric, photosynthetic capital
was consumed.

Over the last ten millennia, crop production has followed similar patterns, although the modes and tempos of agricultural developments have depended on the places where particular cereals were
grown. Crop production can be improved by increasing cultivation area

and yield per hectare per crop per year, eliminating low-yielding crops, reducing post-harvest losses and increasing mechanization. Approximately four millennia ago rises in food production came from increasing the area of arable land through the development of the scratch plough and the ard. Using these inventions man scraped the soil surface in easily worked areas to provide a seedbed for the weedy grasses upon which he survived. Community civil-engineering programmes, such as terracing in Southeast Asia and swamp drainage in the Valley of Mexico, increased the quality and availability of land. Once heavy ploughs and horse collars started to be used, agriculture was extended to the deep, heavy, fertile soils of valley bottoms. Selection of particular cultivars and changes to crop management increased crop yields, whilst better crop storage reduced the amount of harvest lost to pest and diseases. Due to mechanization, land area needed to grow the grasses that fed the animals that powered crop production could be turned over to human food production.

To keep pace with our currently growing population, researchers have estimated that global food production must increase between 70 and 100 per cent before 2050. The vast majority of this will have to come from grasses, and the genes conserved in gene banks.

Rice

Rice feeds more people than any other plant on the planet, but unlike other cereals most rice is grown by the people who consume it. Compared with other cereals, rice is not a significant article of international trade.[6] Different types of rice are adapted to the multiplicity of Asian environments, ranging from the tropics to the temperate latitudes of northern Japan, from the Cambodian lowlands to the Himalayas and from the deep waters of Bangladesh to the dry uplands of Nepal. Consequently, there is tremendous variation in rice characteristics, and the everyday uses and significance of rice in Asian societies.

Rice is an annual grass that can reach more than 1.5 metres in height. There are two main types of rice. The *indica* type has long grains which are not sticky when cooked and is adapted to warm temperate climates. In contrast, the *japonica* type has short, sticky grains and is adapted to damp tropical climates. Typically, seedlings of lowland rice are planted into paddy fields created by the damming and channelling of water. Although not essential for rice cultivation, flooding reduces the necessity for weeding and allows the growth of the nitrogen-fixing fern *Azolla* to fertilize the paddy. Over the last 5,000 years paddy fields have increased in number and area, and today are responsible for up to 30 per cent of the annual man-made emissions of the greenhouse gas methane. Upland rice types rely on high rainfall for their water, whilst deep-water floating rices grow rapidly in waters up to 5 metres deep.

Asian peoples have been dependent on rice as food for at least 9,000 years. As a result, trying to understand the origins of domesticated rice is a challenge. The challenge is made all the greater by the large area of potential rice cultivation, the limited sites for preservation

The etching *Plowing the Ground on which the Rice is to be Sowed, c.* 1775, after Augustin Heckel, showing a bullock plough being pulled through a rice paddy.

of archaeological remains and the difficulties of distinguishing wild rice and cultivated rice in such deposits. The available evidence suggests that *indica*- and *japonica*-type rice diverged well before rice was domesticated; today they cannot interbreed. However, both types interbreed with rice's wild ancestor, *Oryza rufipogon*, a perennial species distributed across Asia. The scientific debate continues about whether domestication happened once or on multiple occasions. The multiple-domestication hypothesis argues that domestication of the *indica* type happened in eastern India and gave rise to rice cultivars with non-sticky long grains, whilst domestication of the *japonica* type occurred in southern China and produced cultivars with sticky short grains.[7] The alternative hypothesis is that rice was domesticated once in the Yangtze Valley of China, followed by subsequent divergence of the *indica* and *japonica* types.[8]

Rice has the smallest genome of any major cereal. The DNA sequence of the whole Asian rice genome was reported in 2005. It was found to be about one-seventh the size of the human genome, with approximately twice as many genes.[9] We only know what a tiny proportion of these genes do. It is rather like having access to a book in a foreign language in which the letters and some of the words can be discerned, but the meanings of the sentences and how they relate to ideas is unknown. One of the genes we do know about is found on the fourth of the twelve chromosomes that make up the rice genome. Grain shattering is an important element of the rice domestication complex. The most significant of the non-shattering genes is called *sh4*. Mutation of a single DNA nucleotide is sufficient to change the protein produced by this gene so that the normal processes of grain shattering do not take place; the mutant rice plant retains grains on the adult.[10]

From southern and East Asia, rice spread throughout the Old World. By the third millennium BC it was expanding into Southeast Asia and across India into Nepal. The classical Greek botanist Theophrastus described rice following Alexander the Great's exped - ition to India. With the rise of the Muslim world, rice extended to the

The Indian Name.

Oryza omnium Autorum, Tourefort. Elem. bot.t.296
Rice.

Sent from Fort St George in the Et Indies, by my bro. D duBois.

Rice collected by
Daniel du Bois at
Fort St George
(modern-day
Chennai), India,
c. 1700, with the
Indian common
name scratched on
a palm leaf label.

southern shores of the Caspian Sea, and by the tenth century the Moors had taken rice to the Iberian Peninsula. The fifteenth century saw rice spread through Italy and France, then into the New World. Rice is not native to the New World, but it became the staple of most of Latin America; it is hardly imaginable to have a meal in Latin America without some combination of rice and beans. The origin of rice in North America appears to be more complex. In the early eighteenth century the colonial south of the United States started to benefit from rice cultivation and the slave trade. Higher prices were paid for slaves who were familiar with rice cultivation in West Africa, leading some academics to place black slaves at the centre of rice culture in colonial and post-colonial America.[11]

It was not only knowledge that the slaves brought with them across the Middle Passage – they also brought rice grains. However, the rice they brought was not Asian rice but African rice, *Oryza glaberrima*, the other economically important rice. African rice appears to have been domesticated about 3,500 years ago from the African rice O. *barthii* in the Upper Niger Delta, from whence it spread across Africa. As in the case of Asian rice, there is an unresolved debate over the single or multiple origins of African rice domestication.[12] African rice has favourable characteristics, including a hard grain and high resistance to diseases and pests. Unfortunately, yields are low and it is difficult to harvest since the grains readily shatter. Following the introduction of Asian rice into the range of African rice, the two coexisted side by side until consumers' preferences decided that it was more economic to grow Asian rather than African rice.[13]

As we have seen, grass domestication and breeding requires appropriate genes to be present in a species. *Zizania*, a genus of four aquatic grasses distributed from eastern India through East Asia and into North America, is commonly known as wild rice. North American wild rice, with its long, black, nutty grains, is naturally distributed in extensive populations from the St Lawrence River to Central Texas. This species was an important part of some North American Amerindian diets, although it was never domesticated.[14] Similarly,

Chippewa women, from the Great Lakes region of North America, harvesting ripe wild rice by beating plants with paddles and collecting the grains in their canoe.

Manchurian rice was gathered from wild stands in ancient China and preferred over Asian rice because of its flavour and nutritional qualities. However, domestication by generations of Chinese farmers proved impossible since the plant's genetic architecture is inappropriate for domestication. Today wild populations of Manchurian rice are rare. However, Manchurian rice is grown and eaten not for the grains but for the shoots, which are often infected with a nutritious, parasitic fungus.[15]

Guarding Food Supplies

Natural characteristics of grains have been used for thousands of years to ensure that crops are planted annually, passed from generation to generation and migrate with humans. In the first two decades of the twentieth century, the Soviet geneticist Nikolai Vavilov was fascinated by the genetics of crop variation and started to explore different regions of the world, collect seeds and store them in vast seed banks in the former Soviet Union; one such was in St Isaac's Square in Leningrad. Vavilov was convinced that the highest amount of crop

Sheaf of modern long-grain rice.

genetic variability was to be found in the areas where crops were first domesticated and where the majority of a crop's close wild relatives were found. In the course of his investigations Vavilov identified centres of crop diversity, including those in the Fertile Crescent, Central Mexico and the Andes.

Vavilov's efforts were about more than discovering crop origins as an intellectual exercise. Seed collections are essential raw materials for improving the resilience of cereals to unknown future hazards, breeding new varieties and resynthesizing crops through conscious selection of particular traits. Seed banks filled with many samples from across a crop's range are arks of variation with the goal of hedging against loss of genetic variation. One of the many stories to emerge from the Nazi's 900 day-long Siege of Leningrad, with its staggering loss of human life, was the dedication shown by some of the custodians of the St Isaac's Square seed collections, who starved rather than eat the grains in the collections.[16] Such stories have stimulated the imaginations of campaigners, journalists, novelists and songwriters, as exemplified in Elise Blackwell's *Hunger* (2003) and by the American folk-rock group The Decemberists in 'When the War Came'. However, the storage of crop genes neither started nor ended with Vavilov. A worldwide network for the storage of both wild and domesticated plants now exists. Two of the most prominent storage facilities are the Millennium Seed Bank, located in southern England, and the Svalbard Global Seed Vault, situated close to the North Pole and carved out of a Norwegian mountain.

Asian rice is one cereal where it is believed that the majority of genetic variation has been captured in seed banks. The rice-seed collection at the International Rice Research Institute, in the Philippines, contains over 100,000 accessions. As rice spread from its centre, or centres, of origin, cycles of hybridization, selection and differentiation led to considerable genetic complexity. We rely on this inherited genetic complexity for breeding new rice cultivars today, and will do so into the foreseeable future.

Traditional approaches to plant breeding involve manipulation of the frequencies of particular genes for useful crop traits through processes of hybridization, and unconscious and conscious selection. This strategy has enabled humans to feed themselves for the last 10,000 years. However, the current challenges posed by climate change, increasing human population and habitat loss have led breeders to consider approaches that involve moving particular genes into crops, or the recreation of crop plants from their component species.

These methods complement traditional breeding approaches. The sources of the genes are the world's seed banks.

Early goals for increasing rice productivity included halving plant height, so that fewer sugars went into stem production and more went into fruit production; producing short, upright leaves, so that sunlight was used more efficiently; and reducing day-length sensitivity, so that plants could be grown and would mature at any time of the year. In 1962 breeders at the recently established International Rice Research Institute took inspiration from the use of 'Norin 10' in wheat. 'Peta', a traditional tall Indonesian variety, was crossed with 'Dee-Geo-Woo-Gen', a Chinese dwarf variety. It was soon discovered that dwarfism was controlled by a single gene, and by the fifth generation of crossing a new variety 'IR-8' was ready for testing. 'IR-8' was officially released in 1966 and yielded up to 10 tonnes of grain per hectare, compared with 1 to 2 tonnes per hectare in traditional varieties. It also produced a crop in 120 days instead of about 180, and remained upright when treated with nitrogen fertilizers. However, 'IR-8' needed artificial fertilizers to be most productive. Despite praise for 'IR-8', some thought the release was premature, while others complained that the grains did not have the same taste and cooking properties as the traditional varieties. More seriously, 'IR-8' was plagued with disease problems such as bacterial blight and tungro virus, and it soon became clear that the focus of rice breeding needed to shift to finding disease and pest resistance.[17]

In 2007 hybrids between African and Asian rice, made by the African Rice Centre, and selected for the harsh, low-input conditions of African agriculture, were hailed by the international press as wonder crops that would lead to the economic resurgence of Africa.[18] However, the yield gains in rice as a consequence of the Green Revolution have all but ceased, and the rate of increase in productivity through improving agricultural practice is slowing. To make the necessary step changes in rice productivity, it has been suggested that rice photosynthesis must be made more efficient. This has led to the radical suggestion that rice must be transformed from a C_3 to a

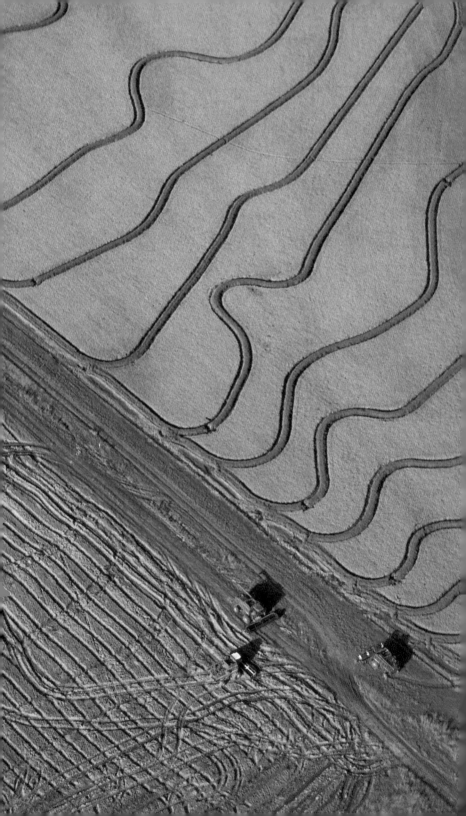

C_4 grass. C_4 plants have evolved on at least 50 separate occasions during the evolution of flowering plants, which implies that, despite the complexities of the necessary morphological and physiological changes, the transition from C_3 to C_4 may be achievable.

Rice is nutritionally incomplete – for example, cleaned rice grains are deficient in vitamins such as A and B_I, and minerals such as iron. Consequently, vitamin-deficiency diseases are frequent in people with rice-dominated diets. Vitamin A deficiency has enormous public health consequences; between 250,000 and 500,000 vitamin-A-deficient children go blind each year, and half of them die within twelve months. However, the nutritional quality of rice can be dramatically changed by enriching it with vitamin A. Strategies for alleviating vitamin A deficiency have met with varying degrees of success, but one proposal has been the development of Golden Rice, which has been achieved by genetically modifying rice to produce high levels of a vitamin A precursor through the introduction of genes from maize and a bacterium. Golden Rice is now being used in Asian rice-breeding programmes.[19]

Critics of crop breeding, often those not facing the direct consequences of lost harvests, have been concerned with health and environmental issues of gene transfer across evolutionary barriers. Others have argued that people's traditional knowledge has been exploited and their biological heritage stolen (biopiracy). Issues of biopiracy are complex and intricate, especially when economically important plants are involved. Simplistic analyses often fail to account for the investment necessary to develop elite crop lines, and store and maintain seeds in gene banks – most of which will never have any commercial value – and the problems of determining appropriate beneficiaries.

Basmati rice has been grown by Indian farmers for thousands of years. However, in 1997 the U.S. Patent and Trademark Office granted a patent on 'Basmati rice lines and grains' to the Texas-based company RiceTec Inc. Understandably, this caused alarm and outrage

opposite: Agroindustrial rice production in Texas.

among Indian farmers and non-governmental organizations, who interpreted the patent as creating a monopoly on basmati rice and restricting imports into the United States. In fact, the patent was for the progeny of a specific rice plant. In a separate case, a group of Californian researchers isolated a bacterial rice-blight resistance gene from rice bred by the International Rice Research Institute using genes introduced from a Malian sample of African rice. The researchers applied for a patent, and were soon surrounded by controversy as a perception developed that the Bela people, holders of traditional knowledge about the original plants, were being exploited.[20]

Feeding a growing human population that has changing expectations of the type of food it wants to eat is a major challenge. Whether scientific agriculture can ensure that food production keeps pace with human population growth remains to be seen. To be most effective, increasing food production must be associated with reductions in both population growth and overall consumption; there must be fewer, slimmer people on the planet.

seven

Sweetening Life

⟨∞⟩

When we consider that the saccharine principle is the soul of
vegetable creation . . . we cannot but admire the partiality of Nature
to the luscious Cane, her favourite offspring, the sublimest effort
of heat and light.

BENJAMIN MOSELEY, *Treatise on Sugar* (1799)

Before the seventeenth century, Europeans had little experience
of concentrated sweetness – the carbohydrate sucrose – and
made do with honey. Sugar was rare and consequently very
expensive in medieval Europe; it was a medicine, spice and condiment
for the extremely rich. Medicines containing ingredients such as
animal faeces and urine were commonplace, and those with money
could have their 'medicine' sweetened with sugar. By the Reformation
the cost of sugar was merely exorbitant, and sugar was used by the very
wealthy to garner influence with the extremely powerful. For example,
in 1591 Edward Seymour, 1st Earl of Hertford, had repeatedly incurred
the displeasure of Elizabeth 1, so he hosted a four-day feast for the
sugar-addicted queen and her court. It included prodigious quantities of elaborate sugar and marzipan sculptures; the ostentatious
displays would have cost the desperate earl a fortune. Eventually sugar
became an everyday preservative, food stuff and sweetener.

About half of the sugar consumed today is extracted from a
perennial grass, sugar cane. It is one of only a small number of

overleaf: Modern sugar cane field in central Brazil.

plants, including sugar beet, sugar maple, sorghum and some palms, which produce sucrose in economically useful quantities. Two centuries ago all commercial sugar came from cane. Over the course of 3,000 years sugar cane had been transformed from a minor plant in the home gardens of Papua New Guineans into a global agro-industrial crop. In the process the Americas, Africa and Europe were changed, and cultures were exterminated and populations enslaved. Furthermore, enormous environmental damage continues to be done today by cane cultivation and sugar extraction. In his darkly comic satire *Strip Tease* (1993), Carl Hiaasen lays bare the social, political and environmental exploitations by the North American sugar-cane industry of the late twentieth century. In this, one finds echoes of earlier sugar-based exploitations in the Caribbean and Latin America.

Saccharum is a genus of about 40 tropical and subtropical grasses, some of which have sweet, pulpy stems; Linnaeus christened the genus thus because of the sweet stems of sugar cane. The sweeter species are chewed in their native areas, while others are important in the breeding of *S. officinarum*, the sugar cane of international trade. Sugar cane, or noble cane, is a complex of high chromosome-number hybrids found only in cultivation; the species cannot persist without cosseting by humans. In New Guinea, where the species probably originated, sugar cane takes centre stage in creation myths and other traditional stories. Sugar-cane stalks are woven into building material, while the leaves are used for roofing and fodder. Furthermore, many named clones, varying in juice sweetness and quantity, stem-fibre content, and leaf and stem colour, are cultivated by the numerous New Guinean tribes.[1]

From New Guinea sugar cane probably travelled as people migrated across Polynesia and into southern and Southeast Asia. By the sixth century sugar cane was being grown in Persia, by the middle of the eighth century it was flourishing in Egypt and by the tenth century it was an important Middle Eastern crop. Arab expansion took sugar cane throughout the Mediterranean as far as the Iberian

Sugar extraction in Dutch Brazil recorded in Piso and Marcgrave's
Historia Naturalis Brasiliae (1648). Slaves are skimming boiling sugar cane
extract, while sugar loaves are piled on the floor.

Peninsula, so that by the fifteenth century the Iberian empires had
introduced cane to Macaronesia, especially Madeira and the Canary
Islands, from whence it was transferred across the Atlantic into the
New World.

The extraction and concentration of sucrose from sugar cane is
a complex, skilled process. Sanskrit texts reveal that crystallized sugar
was being extracted in northern India during the first millennium
BC, where there was a tradition of extracting palm sugar.[2] The basic
elements of the process have not changed, although the details of
modern sugar extraction are radically different from those of the
eighteenth century.

Juice squeezed from the cane stem is boiled. Lime is added to the
boiling juice, and the scum of insoluble material and soluble non-
sugars is removed. Sucrose crystallizes as the concentrated syrup cools
and the molasses drain away. Sugar nomenclature is diverse, and
depends on the manufacturing process and the amount of molasses in
the final product. Unrefined brown sugars bear evocative names such
as demerara, muscovado, Barbados, rapadura and panela. In 1746 the
English historian Thomas Salmon preferred white, more refined sugar:

> The sugar of this country [Brazil] is much better than that
> which we bring home from our plantations: For all the sugar

that is made here is clay'd, which makes it whiter and finer than our muscovado, as we call our unrefin'd sugar. Our planters seldom refine any with clay, unless sometimes a little to send home as presents to their friends in England.[3]

Sugar-cane Biology

In the late 1780s John Sibthorp, Sherardian Professor of Botany at Oxford University, with sugar cane in hand, presumably grown in the Botanic Garden, told his undergraduate students studying botany:

> The Plant from which Sugar is prepared by a particular Process is a Sort of Grass. . . . We have here this Plant the S[accharum]. officinale but it is not in flower. We observe however from the flat appearance of its leaves that it is a Sort of Grass. It is a Native of both Indies & in respect to its Economical Uses may be considered as a Grass of the first Importance[4]

Understanding sugar-cane biology is important to understanding its production. However, the sons of empire attending Sibthorp's lecture gained little knowledge of sugar cane, despite West Indian sugar being the basis of British wealth.

The sugar-cane stem is packed with sucrose-filled, pulpy cells. Just as starch is the energy store of cereal grains, so sucrose is the energy store of sugar cane. Cane stems are up to 6 metres long and are composed of a series of near-identical segments. Each segment, which can be up to 25 centimetres long and 6 centimetres in diameter, has a bud, a rooting region and a ring of growing tissue. Above-ground segments are long and produce razor-edged leaves up to 1.2 metres long and 10 centimetres wide. In contrast, below-ground segments are short, with scale-like leaves, roots and buds that develop into tillers. The outside of the stem is hard and covered in wax. Genetically, the many clonal cultivars vary in segment length, diameter, shape and colour. However, these features are also modified by environmental conditions such as light and nitrogen levels.

Cane fields are planted using stem segments (or setts), with some 9,000 to 14,000 setts planted in an area the size of a football pitch. As a sett grows and produces a horizontal underground stem (rhizome) and roots, the sugar store is used. Once the rhizome has fully developed, leaves emerge above ground and the cane starts to produce its own sugars. The stem elongates rapidly, the number of segments produced being determined by the cultivar, climate and growing conditions. Other rhizome buds develop so that clumps of stems are produced. Walking along tracks in a commercial cane field, walls of densely packed cane stems rise on both sides, with bright green leaves at the stem top and yellowing leaves lower down. One is left with the impression of walking through a giant lawn.

In young stems sugars are in the form of fructose and glucose, but as the cane ripens the sugars are modified and stored as sucrose. After ten to 24 months, sucrose content is at its maximum and the cane is harvested. If a stem is not harvested, the sucrose is used when the stem flowers, after which the stem dies. Once harvested, new stems

Parham Hill House and sugar plantation, Antigua, together with slaves and overseer.

(ratoons) grow, which are in turn harvested. Sucrose levels are gradually reduced with each ratoon harvest, so eventually it becomes economic to grub up the cane clumps and replant the whole field. In parts of Barbados the same land has been used for sugar-cane planting for more than 300 years.

The best harvests are produced on well-drained soils in regions with long, warm growing seasons and plenty of sunlight, water and fertilizer. Furthermore, because flowering reduces sucrose levels ingenious methods have been invented to prevent flowering, including lighting the fields briefly at night with burning magnesium and aluminium, reducing water and increasing nitrogen input. Harvest is limited to the few months when sucrose contents are at their highest, but must be highly coordinated, since sucrose levels decline within two days of harvest. Once an entirely manual process, harvesting today is highly mechanized. Like icebreakers, modern, caterpillar-tracked cane harvesters push their way through cane fields, peeling away layer after layer of cane stalks. The green cane tops, with their low sucrose content, are removed before cutting plates slice the stems close to the ground. As the cut stems pass though the harvester they are chopped into convenient segments for milling before being tossed into trailers. Of course, as the harvesters pass, mammals are mashed and reptiles ripped apart, and raptors circle in the cane combine's wake.

Sugar cane is vulnerable to a gamut of bacterial, viral and fungal diseases and pests. Because it is a clonal plant grown in high-density tropical and subtropical monocultures, any diseases spread rapidly. In the second half of the nineteenth century disease outbreaks in many sugar cane-growing regions almost eliminated 'Bourbon', the most widely cultivated sugar cane variety, as an economic crop.[5] The industry was rescued by resistant cultivars developed by the activities of plant breeders. Rats follow humans around the globe and, unsurprisingly, are common in cane fields. They weaken sugar-cane stems, spread pathogens and destroy tillers. In the late nineteenth century, in an attempt to control rats in West Indian cane fields, mongooses were introduced from India. However, the mongooses found native mammals and birds easier to prey on than rats; the effort failed.[6]

Sugar Cane and People

Sugar production is capital intensive; it requires land and equipment for milling and refining. A field the size of a football pitch produces about 50 tonnes of sugar cane, equivalent to some 6.5 tonnes of refined sugar, the average annual sugar consumption of 170 Europeans. If the demand for sugar is to be supplied, it must be accepted that sugar cane, a 'pleasant and profitable reed',[7] will make great demands on the growers and the environment.

Land must be deforested, large amounts of water used and high levels of fertilizer applied to make cane fields productive. Furthermore, planting and fertilizing fields, harvesting cane and extracting sugar are labour-intensive processes. Consequently, sugar-cane history is one of human exploitation and environmental destruction, in which slavery played a significant role. Much has been written about slavery and its legacy; the North American slave crops of tobacco and cotton, and the Caribbean and Latin American slave crop of sugar, have been prominent in these accounts.

Sugar cane was introduced from the Canary Islands to the New World by Christopher Columbus on his second voyage in 1493. Columbus supervised the cane planting on Hispaniola (present-day Dominican Republic) and was amazed at the rapidity with which the plant grew. Hispaniola was populated by approximately three million indigenous agriculturalists, the Taino, but agriculture was not a major concern for the new settlers; they wanted the immediate reward of gold. By 1542, Bartolomé de las Casas, the chronicler of Spanish abuses in the West Indies, recorded only 200 Taino. Within two decades the Taino were extinct, wiped out by the deadly combination of forced labour, religious dogma, bigotry and imported diseases such as smallpox, measles, cholera and influenza.[8] Today all that remains of Taino culture are isolated

James Gillray, cartoon ridiculing the sugar boycott adopted
by George III's household, 1792.

objects in museums and the descriptions in *A Short History of the
Destruction of the Indies* (1552) and *General History of the Indies*, both by
Las Casas. The Taino were among the first victims of American
sugar-cane cultivation.

Las Casas, an influential slave owner and sugar planter in his
own right, did what he thought was best to protect the indigenous
people of the West Indies. He supported the proposal by Spanish
sugar planters to replace indigenous slaves by African ones. The
road to hell is paved with good intentions, and the proposal supported by Las Casas was the thin end of a wedge. Eventually, African
slaves were adopted by the Iberian and British Empires across the
Americas, and the Triangular Trade among Britain, West Africa and
the Caribbean emerged.

Without a slave-labour force, economic sugar production would
have been impossible. In 1799 the English plantation doctor and sugar
enthusiast Benjamin Moseley succinctly summarized the position:

If Jamaica, and the other English sugar islands, were to share the fate of *St. Domingue* [Haiti], by the horrors of war, a distress would arise, not only in England, but in Europe, not confined to the present generation, but that would descend to the child unborn. Of such importance has the agriculture of half a million of Africans, become to Europeans.[9]

Sugar cane grows best in areas with high temperatures and rainfall, and rich, deep soils; the areas where manual labour is most difficult and physically draining. Once areas had been cleared, fields were planted by cane-holing during the wet season. Three gangs of field slaves worked together. The first gang made a hole in the heavy soil, the second gang planted a cane sett and the third made sure that the area was clear of weeds. With up to 20,000 setts planted per hectare, this was backbreaking work. Furthermore, fertilizers such as animal manure and other waste had to be carted to the fields. Draught animals needed to be fed, so fodder collected from areas that had not been converted to cane fields was supplemented with the scum skimmed from the tops of the sugar cauldrons. During the wet season feeding animals may have been relatively straightforward, but during the dry season, as vegetation died back, this became an increasingly difficult task. Burning fields at the start of the cane harvest removed unwanted cane leaves and drove away, at least temporarily, the snakes and other vermin that filled the fields. The air would be filled with wisps of black soot and the acrid stench of burned sugar, whilst the canes were caked with soot and caramelized sugar. Sweating, soot-caked slaves hacked at the canes with cutlasses or machetes. Cut too far from the ground and the sucrose-rich stem base was lost; cut too close and ratoons of the next year's crop would be lost. Under the whip to cut as much cane as possible, injuries were very high. Underfed and abused cutters might be expected to harvest 3 to 4 tonnes of cane per day in a hot, sticky climate. Wielding a machete is a skilled business and horrific accidents were not uncommon; there were no shin and forearm guards for these workers.

Once the cane had been hauled back to the mill, slaves specializing in sugar extraction took over. In 1597, using information he got from his Indian servant, the herbalist John Gerard reported that:

> in some places they use a great wheele, wherein slaves do tread and walke as dogs do a turning the spit: and some others do feed as it were the bottome of the said wheele, wherein are some sharpe or hard things which do cut and crush the Canes into powder.[10]

By the eighteenth century many mills were driven by animals or water, but they were still hand-fed. A moment's inattention and slaves would lose their hands, if they were lucky. Voltaire's horrified hero in *Candide* (1759) reports meeting a double-amputee slave on the side of a Surinamese road:

> when we work in the sugar refineries and catch our finger in the mill, they cut off the hand: when we try to run way, they cut off a leg: both things have happened to me. It is at this price that you eat sugar in Europe.[11]

The bagasse (cane waste), and the wood stripped from forests, was fed to the furnaces that heated the fuel-hungry sugar cauldrons. In the refining rooms the temperature was always high and the atmosphere was stifling, as the sticky syrup was concentrated by boiling. According to Moseley, an imperial ton of good-quality cane could be expected to produce 1,041 5/16 pounds of double and single refined sugar, 448 pounds of piece sugar, 224 pounds of scale or bastard sugar, 498 pounds of molasses or treacle and 28 11/16 pounds of scum and dirt.[12] However, to get these yields, and better, plantation owners were dependent on the skills of the slaves involved in the refining process. A good sugar-refining slave was a great asset.

Descriptions of cane fields and sugar production presented to European audiences merely described processes and emphasized

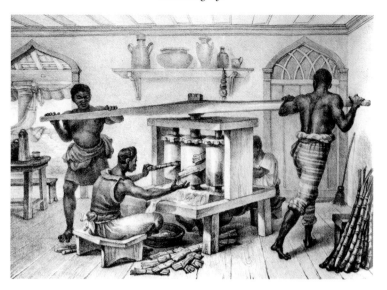

Jean-Baptiste Debret's *Petit moulin a sucre portatif* (1835) showing slaves in
Rio de Janeiro, Brazil, extracting juice from sugar cane.

economic benefits. Some of these sanitized descriptions, and the
images that accompanied them, were even romanticized. The sweat,
grime, blood, disease, emaciation, degradation and barbarity of life in
the cane fields were omitted. Some artists did try to give a sense of what
slavery meant. In Europe images of Brazilian slavery were found in
Jean-Baptiste Debret's *Voyage Pittoresque et Historique au Brésil* ('A
Picturesque and Historic Voyage to Brazil', 1834–9) and Johann
Moritz Rugendas's *Voyage Pittoresque dans le Brésil* ('Picturesque Voyage
to Brazil', 1835). These artists presented their rich, educated publics
with graphic lithographs of slaves in chains and spiked iron collars, or
bound and naked and being flogged with cat-of-five-tails or beaten
with whips designed to flay victims. However disturbing these images,
particularly in combination with Debret's descriptive text, these too
were sanitized compared with the original sketches. Debret, in his published lithograph *L'execution de la punition du fouet* ('Execution of the
Punishment of the Whip') with its three slaves trapped by their
ankles in stocks, omits a fourth slave who, in the associated watercolour,
is held in the stocks by his head. Debret's uncoloured lithograph

Unknown artist, *Family Being Served with Tea, c.* 1745.

Feitors corrigeant des nègres ('Plantation Overseers Disciplining Blacks') omits the bloody wounds on the naked slave's buttocks and the bloodstains on the bullock whip that an overseer uses to beat a slave.[13] Every sugar consumer was complicit in the slavery.

By the end of the eighteenth century the morality of the slave trade was being questioned, but it was not until the early nineteenth century that laws were put in place which outlawed slavery in the British Empire. This did not stop British companies from exploiting slavery in countries where it remained legal. For example, the directors of the British-owned St John d'El Rey Mining Company, which was dependent on Brazilian slave labour, defended their position before the British Parliament into the late 1840s.[14] When Charles Darwin, a committed abolitionist and member of the Wedgwood family, left Brazilian shores on board the *Beagle* on 19 August 1836, he bluntly stated: 'I thank God, I shall never again visit a slave-country.'[15] Slavery was finally abolished in Brazil in 1888. What took the place of cane-field slaves in many countries was slavery by another name – indentured labour.

Sugar is sold in numerous purities and grain sizes: dark and light muscovado sugar; demerara and white sugar; caster and icing sugar.

Britain was but one of many European powers in the eight-eenth and nineteenth centuries whose populaces were addicted to sugar and the profits that rolled in on the backs of slaves and indentured labour. Sugar not only killed the producers; it killed its consumers, albeit sweetly and silently. In traditional Fijian culture, sugar-cane spears killed directly. Today sugar's killing power is more subtle through obesity, Type 2 diabetes and heart disease, not to mention bad teeth. In Europe sugar was regarded as a medicine. Although some made the connection between sugar consumption and the pissing evil (diabetes), the effects of sugar on teeth were dismissed as little more than 'a prudent old woman's bug-bear, to frighten children'.[16]

In Gerard's time few British people could afford sugar even sold by the ounce; a century later most people could afford it sold by the pound. When Henry Somerset, first Duke of Beaufort, died in 1700 at the age of 70, he

> was opened; his viscera were found . . . as perfect as in a person of twenty: with his teeth white, and firm. He had for forty years before his death used a pound of sugar daily, in his wine, chocolate, and sweet-meats.[17]

Britain's per-capita sugar consumption has increased ever since, often disguised in all manner of unlikely foods.

Sugar made Britain's fortune in the seventeenth and eighteenth centuries. The British appetite for sugar appeared insatiable. West Indian sugar indirectly funded the development of cities such as Liverpool and Bristol, the establishment of the Royal Botanic Gardens, Kew, and no end of buildings in London. West Indian cane plantations also provided a convenient place for younger sons of the landed gentry and members of the emerging middle class to make their fortunes. Sugar made beverages such as tea, coffee and chocolate palatable, leading to the rise of the tea and coffee shops as meeting places for political, artistic and scientific debate. The cultural stereotype of

Britain as a nation of sweet-tea drinkers was born during the nineteenth century. Indeed, workers employed in factories during the Industrial Revolution sometimes appear to have survived on little except bread, butter and sweet tea.[18]

Eventually, all things change. During the seventeenth century Brazil dominated the world sugar market, but by the eighteenth century West Indian plantations dominated. Today, Brazil is once again the world's single most important sugar-cane producer. So important is sugar cane in Brazil that the sociologist Gilberto de Mello Freyre argued that sugar is at the root of Brazil's complex socio-cultural life.[19] Because of the cultural significance of sugar one of the prominent mountains near Rio de Janeiro, which reminded Portuguese colonizers of a sugar loaf, was called Pão d'Açúcar (Sugar Loaf).

The supremacy of sugar cane as a sugar source was challenged as Napoleon successfully promoted sugar beet in the early nineteenth century. Today both sugar cane and sugar beet face competition from the corn syrup extracted from grasses such as sorghum and maize. Sugar-cane production has been given a new boost by the promise it offers as a source of raw material for the production of biofuels, especially alcohol.

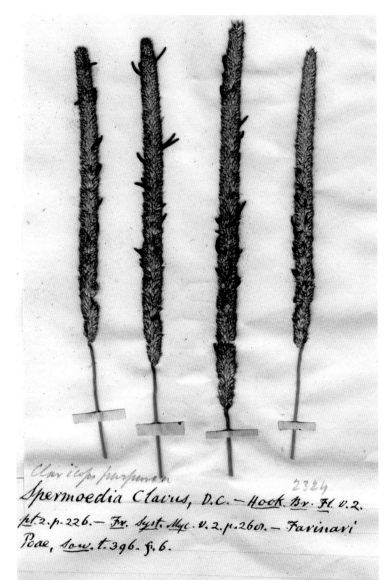

Clariceps purpurea

2324

Spermoedia Clavus, D.C. — Hook. Br. Fl. v.2. pt.2.p.226. — Fr. Syst. Myc. v.2.p.260. — Farinari Poae, Sow. t.396. f.6.

Common Ergot. — On *Phleum pratense*, and on various other Gramineae, Oxf. Gard. Sepr 11. 1846.

Ergot infecting timothy grass collected in the Oxford Botanic Garden in 1846.

eight

Protecting the Crop

Barley is more liable to it [rust] than wheat; while of barleys some kinds are more liable than others . . . Moreover the position and character of the land make no small difference in this respect; for lands which are exposed to the wind and elevated are not liable to rust, or less so, while those that lie low and are not exposed to the wind are more so.

THEOPHRASTUS, *Enquiry Into Plants*

The Roman poet Virgil warns of the 'baneful mildew feeding on the stems' of wheat.[1] Cereal grains infected with hallucinogenic fungi were used in the sacred rituals of ancient Greece.[2] The Romans, like the Greeks, were familiar with the diseases of their cereals, if not their causes. In the Roman calendar 25 April was Robigalia, a festival for the protection of grain fields dedicated to Robigus, the personification of agricultural disease; the sacrifice was the blood and guts of an unweaned puppy.[3] Ovid reports the necessary invocations to the deity:

thou scaly Mildew, spare the sprouting corn, and let the smooth top quiver on the surface of the ground. O let the crops, nursed by the stars of a propitious sky, grow till they are ripe for the sickle. No feeble power is thine . . . O spare, I pray, and take thy scabby hands from off the harvest![4]

The ancients knew how to control cereal diseases, even without disembowelling canids. Plant the right cereal variety in the right place, and do not overwater; similar advice is regularly offered to gardeners on Radio 4's *Gardeners' Question Time*.

Crop disease has been accompanied by famine throughout recorded history. Annually, cereal crops are bombarded with pathogens of all descriptions – viruses, bacteria and fungi, even excluding pests such as nematodes, insects, birds and mammals. In 1970 a fungal epidemic, southern corn leaf blight, resulted in the loss of 15 per cent of maize production in the United States.[5] The epidemic started in Florida and moved north, but only affected maize containing a particular set of genes. Unfortunately, these genes had been used widely in maize breeding, so the disease affected most of the U.S. Corn Belt; in this case the only losses were financial. Other cereal diseases, such as rice blast fungus, have the potential to cast vast areas of the developing world into famine.

The convulsive and gangrenous symptoms of St Anthony's Fire (ergotism), named after the patron saint of epilepsy, fire and infection, have been known in Europe since the Middle Ages.[6] Epidemics of ergotism periodically swept parts of northern Europe where rye was cultivated and consumed. One of the most notorious epidemics happened in AD 994, in Aquitaine, when approximately 40,000 people died.[7] In 1676 the French botanist Daniel Dodart advised the French Academy that if St Anthony's Fire was to be controlled, ergot must be removed from rye grains.[8] In 1764 the German botanist Baron Otto von Münchhausen argued that ergot was a fungal infection, but this controversial conclusion was only finally accepted in the 1850s, when ergot's life cycle was demonstrated.[9]

Ergot-infected cereal ears have hard, narrow, dark 'spurs' (sclerotia) that replace some or all of the grains; the name ergot refers specifically to these 'dormant spurs'.[10] Ergot is more frequently found in rye than in other cultivated cereals such as wheat. In contrast to most cereals cultivated in Europe, rye is cross pollinated, hence the flowers open and are likely to be exposed to ergot spores. Ergot sclerotia contain two powerful hallucinogenic and toxic alkaloids; the hallucinogen LSD was originally synthesized from ergot. As a result of the realization that rye consumption was linked to ergotism, the despised millers, who were usually portrayed as corrupt, were forced to grind clean grain and sell pure flour. This reduced the frequency of European ergotism epidemics dramatically. The rarity of ergotism in Britain was explained – the British had no taste for rye. The hallucinogenic effects of ergot have naturally led some scholars to link it to the persecution of so-called witches, especially in northern Europe. In the case of the Scottish witch persecutions of the late fifteenth to mid-sixteenth centuries, associations with ergotism have been rejected since rye was not a Scottish staple.[11] It has been contentiously argued that the Salem witch accusations in New England in 1692 were linked to ergotism.[12]

Epidemics affecting grasses have also been used as plot devices in some works of science fiction. John Christopher, in his novel *The Death of Grass* (1956), conceived a world where a virus laid waste all the world's grasses. Global society collapsed as cereals and pasture lands disappeared, people without potatoes starved and the British government took drastic action to reduce the country's population. The people in Christopher's world soon discovered their absolute reliance on grasses as food.

Grass populations are not only under attack from microbiological pathogens; they are also assailed by hemiparasitic plants such as witchweed and eyebright, and parasitic plants like broomrape and dodder. Hemiparasitic plants produce their own sugars by photosynthesis, but get water and other nutrients from a host. In contrast, parasites get all of their needs from a host and have no chlorophyll. Witchweeds, with their vivid, toadflax-like flowers, are annual root parasites of the Old World tropics and subtropics, introduced into the New World. Witchweed is devastating to the yields of crops such as millet, maize and sorghum in 40 million hectares of sub-Saharan African. Unfortunately, the subsistence farmers who sustain these losses are poorly equipped to weather them, and to invest in expensive control measures. Despite the fact that some African sorghums, millets and maizes are resistant to witchweed, control is difficult because vast numbers of tiny seeds are produced each year, which remain dormant in the soil for years. Since host roots produce chemicals called strigolactones that promote seed germination,[13] if infestations are to be controlled they must be detected before germination.

Tackling Disease

The approximately 630 million tons of bread wheat produced annually feed more than 4.5 billion people.[14] Furthermore, to feed the increasing demand for bread wheat in the developing world, it is estimated that 60 per cent more wheat must be produced by 2050. Consequently, fungi that reduce yield will have catastrophic effects. One such disease today is black stem rust, caused by the parasitic fungus *Puccinia graminis*.

For centuries European farmers recognized a link between barberry in the hedges around their fields and the occurrence of black stem rust on their cereal crops.[15] However, barberry, a spiny native shrub of hedges around European wheat fields, was also valued as a medicinal plant and a source of yellow dye.[16] In about 1660 the French promulgated the Edict of Rouen, which required the destruction of barberry in areas where wheat was grown.[17] The English introduced barberry to colonial America at about the same time as a hedging plant, but by the mid-eighteenth century three New England colonies (Connecticut, Massachusetts and Rhode Island) had passed laws to eliminate the shrub from cereal-growing areas.[18] By the early nineteenth century laws requiring barberry eradication were popping up across Europe. Yet in 1858 the pomologist Robert Hogg asserted that 'the popular delusion . . . Berberry communicates blight to grain crops is entirely without foundation'.[19] Less than a decade later, the

Field experiments are essential for breeding grasses for resistance against fungal disease.

German mycologist Anton de Bary demonstrated unequivocally that the fungus responsible for cereal rust required barberry to complete its complex life cycle;[20] there was a scientific basis for Hogg's 'popular delusion' after all.

Black stem rust has spores that are readily carried by wind, insects, water droplets and humans. In 1998 a highly virulent rust strain (Ug99) emerged in Uganda.[21] In just over a decade, Ug99 has spread to the East African highlands, Zimbabwe, South Africa, Sudan, Yemen and as far as Iran. Ug99 is now a major threat to global wheat production because the vast majority of bread-wheat cultivars grown worldwide are susceptible.

Modern farmers are familiar with fighting cereal disease, often through integrating different weapons in their armouries. Crop-management practices combined with cultivars containing resistance genes and fungicide application are important. Disease spread can be reduced by growing many different cultivars of a crop, with each cultivar carrying different resistance genes; monocultures of the same genetic type must be avoided. Farmers in China improve resistance to rice blast fungus by growing several different rice varieties in the same field.[22]

The resistance genes found in traditional cultivars have formed the basis of plant breeding, although today there is great interest in being able to introduce genes into crops from species with which they would not usually mate, using genetic modification (GM) appro-aches.[23] However, in Europe, following the furore created by the naive, inept marketing of GM maize imports at the end of the 1990s, there is considerable resistance to GM.[24] In the late twentieth century 'greener' alternatives, based on growing old crop cultivars, and using biological control and other 'green' practices, became fashionable in some developed economies.

In the case of black stem rust, management practices can help to reduce infection, but the fungicides are usually not economic to use as a matter of routine. Furthermore, there is increasing concern over the environmental longevity of fungicide and pesticide residues. The best line of defence again black stem rust is the use of cultivars that contain resistance genes. Stem rust resistance genes are found in bread wheat; some occur naturally, while others have been introduced through hybridization and breeding from other grasses such as einkorn, rye and intermediate wheatgrass.[25] Unfortunately, Ug99 has virulence against the most effective stem rust resistance gene. After searching some 200,000 accessions from international seed banks, Ug99 resistance has been found in some bread-wheat samples, and these genes are being bred into susceptible bread wheats. However, major issues now have to be faced about how these resistance alleles are to be transferred into popular wheat varieties and how farmers will be encouraged to use the new cultivars.

All major cereal crops are attacked by hundreds of different diseases, and these are constantly evolving. Constant vigilance is therefore required by farmers and plant breeders if the worst effects of plant pathogens are to be kept at bay. Besides being major causes of grass disease, fungi are important for the release and transport of nutrients in grasslands, and for the fermentation of grass-derived sugars into alcohol.

Decay and Transport

Death is as important a biological process as birth. Consequently, if grasslands are not to be buried under tonnes of straw and depleted of important nutrients, plants must be broken down and the chemicals that make up their bodies salvaged. The biological recyclers are microbes such as bacteria and fungi, and they do their work for the most part unseen and unremarked. For most of the year such fungi are only visible in the soil and leaf litter as microscopic, gossamer networks that secrete enzymes which break down the dead plants. However, as summer draws to a close, and temperatures drop and the air becomes more humid, temperate grasslands are transformed. Fungi throw up their reproductive bodies in the form of the familiar mushrooms and toadstools. Carmine, yellow and pink waxcaps,

Fungal fairy ring on Welsh clifftop grassland.

purple fairy clubs and pinwheel-like Japanese parasols, along with the white, skull-like form of the giant puffball, so aptly named *tête de mort* in France, vie for attention. Many fungi are dotted here and there, while others huddle together in clumps and some form fairy rings. However, the macroscopic fungi are merely a small selection of the myriad of microscopic fungi that are never visible to the casual observer.

Among the microscopic fungi are those that form intimate mutual - istic associations (mycorrhizae, literally 'fungus roots') with the roots of grassland and arable grasses. Below ground plants encounter as much competition as above ground. Therefore mechanisms that increase the acquisition of scarce essential mineral nutrients are highly advantageous. The importance of the mycorrhizal association for plants can be seen by the evolution of such associations soon after the emergence of plants onto the land.[26] In grasses part of the fungus enters cells of the root, forming specialized balloon- and tree-like structures; 85 per cent of plant families have such mycorrhizae.[27] The advantage for the fungus is direct access to carbohydrates from the plant. The advantage for the grass is an increase in the efficiency of water and nutrient uptake, hence they are able to colonize poor soils. Furthermore, evidence is emerging that the high diversity of mycorrhizal fungi in grasslands may afford protection to grasses from pathogens.[28] Modern agricultural practices such as high nitrate and phosphate inputs and regular ploughing appear to inhibit mycorrhizae formation. Consequently, the suggestion has been made that cereal crops could be made more productive simply by considering the needs of mycorrhizal fungi in the soil ecosystem.[29]

More dramatic still is the association between fungi that live inside the cells of Geyser panic grass, which grows in the hot soils of Yellowstone National Park, USA. For the grass and the fungus to survive together at high temperatures, the fungus must be infected by a particular virus.[30] Similar associations have also been reported from another grass of extreme environments, Antarctic hairgrass.[31]

Yeast and Fermentation

Fermentation is the process that converts carbohydrates to alcohols and carbon dioxide, and ultimately to organic acids. Ethanol, the simple two-carbon alcohol people consume, only needs a sugar source, an anaerobic environment and the yeast fungus for its production. Humans have produced ethanol for thousands of years.[32] Indeed, there are suggestions that barley was first domesticated for beer production.[33] However, it was not until 1856 that the French chemist Louis Pasteur made the connection between yeast and fermentation.[34]

All manner of grasses have been used for alcohol manufacture either by simple fermentation or with the additional step of distillation to concentrate ethanol and produce spirits. Fermented barley

Pre-Sagonic, clay cuneiform tablet recording the distribution of barley rations.

grains become beer and ale, which when distilled become malt whisky. Wheat grains are fermented to produce wheat beer, but more importantly distilled for vodka. Rye grains are used to make rye beer or whisky, while maize kernels become *chica* in Central and South America and bourbon in North America. In Africa sorghum and millet grains are fermented to produce beer, and in Southeast Asia rice is brewed to make rice beers such as sake. Sugar cane is a major source of distilled spirits such as rum in the Caribbean and *cachaça* in Brazil. The cultures that have developed around alcoholic drinks, for example beer, whisky, sake and *cachaça*, are replete with their own languages, rituals and mysteries, which to the outsider verge on the fetishistic.[35]

The British folk song 'John Barleycorn' anthropomorphizes the agricultural cycle, the central role of barley in beer and whisky making, and its importance in everyday life, often as a social stereotype; 'The huntsman he can't hunt the fox nor so loudly to blow his horn / And the tinker he can't mend kettles nor pots without a little barleycorn'. John Barleycorn had a more sinister part in the cult film *The Wicker Man* (1973), where barley bread moulded into human form is referred to as 'the life of the fields'.

Alcohol, fermented or distilled, from grasses or non-grasses, is a double-edged sword and has well-known social effects.[36] Exchequers that tax alcohol accrue vast sums from its sale, but must cope with its effects on the behaviour and health of their populations. Before the early twentieth century, and the ready availability of clean water, beer was seen as a drink free from water-borne diseases.[37] In 1751 the cartoonist and printmaker William Hogarth published two prints, *Beer Street* and *Gin Lane*, in direct support of the Gin Act 1751. *Beer Street* denizens are happy, responsible, hardworking citizens, while those of *Gin Lane* are unhappy, feckless and lazy. The messages are clear: it matters what and when you drink; British beer, good – foreign spirits, bad.[38] English literature is peppered with memorable alcoholics; the grotesque Sairey Gamp in Dickens's *Martin Chuzzlewit* (1843–4), the abusive Arthur Huntingdon in Anne Brontë's *The Tenant of Wildfell Hall* (1848), the tactless Sir Roger Scatcherd in Trollope's *Doctor Thorne* (1858) and the spoiled Lord Sebastian Flyte in Waugh's *Brideshead Revisited* (1945). In response to people's alcohol problems in nineteenth-century Britain, the temperance movement was born and took on tea culture as its drug of choice, just as the Islamic world had taken on coffee culture.[39]

George Gardner, the Scottish explorer of nineteenth-century Brazil and critic of *cachaça* use, considered that the ill-health of Brazilians was due to their diet of beans and maize meal, combined with an 'immoderate use of rum'.[40] However, he acknowledged that Brazilians were temperate compared with the Liverpudlians he encountered when he returned to Britain in 1841. Thirty years later the explorer

William Hogarth's *Gin Lane*, 1751, showing the
debauching effects of distilled alcohol.

Richard Burton described the heroic consumption of *cachaça* by Brazilian
men, which led to 'dropsy and death', and 'delirium tremens and an early
grave' in foreigners. Burton's only use for *cachaça* was for 'bathing after
insolation' and relieving the 'discomfort of insect bites'.[41] Naturalists
also found it useful for preserving dead animals.[42]

Besides ethanol, the other product of fermentation is carbon
dioxide, the essential component of leavened bread. Like beer, bread
is a simple product; it is made by mixing water with flour and a leav-

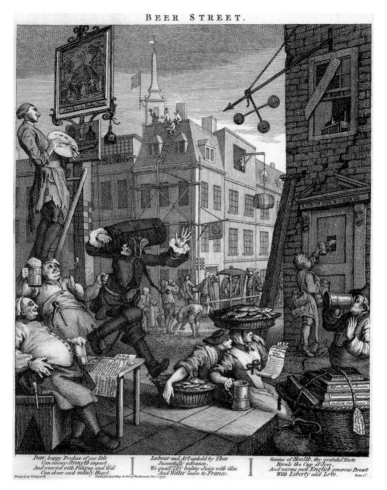

William Hogarth's *Beer Street*, 1751, showing the
calming effects of brewed alcohol.

ening agent. The leavening agent is usually yeast, but may also be an
inorganic chemical such as sodium bicarbonate. Flour for leavened
bread must have a high protein content so that gluten forms. Gluten
molecules trap the carbon dioxide released by fermentation to produce airy dough. Wheat flour is particularly rich in proteins, and particular cultivars, with very high protein contents, are grown for bread
making. Other cereal grains, for example rye, maize and oats, have very
low protein contents and are therefore not used in leavened bread.

Leavened bread.

If fermentation occurs in aerobic conditions, bread and beer sour because of the formation of organic acids. The most significant of these acids is vinegar, which can be used for food preservation and the manufacture of myriads of other useful chemicals. Cereal grains are more than food; they become the raw materials for the chemical industries.

nine

Foraging the Fields

Whoever has limestone land has blue grass; whoever has blue grass
has the basis of all agricultural prosperity; and that man, if he have
not the finest horses, cattle, and sheep, has no one to blame but himself. Others, in other circumstances, may do well. He can hardly
avoid doing well, if he will try.

CHARLES LOUIS FLINT, *Grasses and Forage Plants* (1859)

I mages of human populations eking out an existence foraging for
grasses and leaves are unfortunately familiar and powerful por-
traits of poverty and famine. Humans are not natural grazers,
but rely on grazing animals for meat and dairy products – by-products
of grasses harvesting starlight. Furthermore, before the invention of
the internal combustion engine, horses, mules, oxen and camels were
the world's transport and heavy agricultural labour. At the end of the
nineteenth century at least 200,000 draught horses were used in
London and Westminster;[1] there were thousands more across Britain.
In 2010 the FAO reported that more than 3.7 trillion asses, buffaloes,
camels, cattle, goats, horses, mules and sheep provided food, transport and fertilizer for humans.[2] Today the majority of farming is
mechanized, powered by prehistoric starlight trapped by plants before
grasses evolved.

Animals must be fed, no matter how humans choose to exploit
them. Consequently, there are intimate bonds among the lives of
grasses, livestock and humans: no grass, no livestock; no livestock, no

Harvested oats around Oxford in the 1920s.

manure; no manure, no grass. Fodder incurs the most significant economic cost of using animals, since both labour and land are needed for
its production. When animals are used casually or stocking densities
are low, livestock can usually fend for itself by scavenging, grazing and
browsing. As animals are made more productive, large amounts of
high-quality food (such as cereal grains and pasture) are needed.
Samuel Johnson, in his *Dictionary* (1755), defined oats as 'a grain, which
in England is generally given to horses, but in Scotland supports the
people'.[3] Often taken as a slur on the Scots, the statement emerges
from the social cachet associated with wheat and the ancient belief
that wheat degenerated into oats over time. It failed to recognize oats
as a quality cereal grain that sustained all Britain's rural poor, and her
horses. Only by the close of the eighteenth century was wheat an
affordable food for most Britons; one century later maize became a major
animal feed.[4]

Grass as Forage

Agriculturally, forage is any plant material that is used to feed domesticated herbivores. However, ecologically herbivores include the many thousands of species supported by natural grasslands, ranging from large charismatic mammals such as wildebeest, bison and wild horses, to multitudes of insects such as a crickets, beetles and bugs. The quality of forage is determined by its nutrient content, the amount of energy grazers gain from it (digestibility) and the chemicals produced when it is digested. Forage nutrients include minerals, structural (cell-wall) and non-structural (starch, sugars, organic acids) carbohydrates, proteins and fats.

As might be expected some grasses have higher forage value than others. For example, the wiry-leaved mat grass of British moorlands is almost inedible, whilst in damp lowlands perennial ryegrass is highly prized. With more sunlight and a longer growing season, tropical grasses might be expected to make better forage than temperate ones. However, temperate grasses are generally more digestible than tropical ones. Cell-wall digestibility decreases as temperature increases, and there is greater accumulation of digestible storage products at low temperatures than at high temperatures.

Grasses are seasonal in their growth patterns, even in the tropics. When temperatures in Britain fall below 5°C grasses hardly grow at all, but they grow vigorously in warm, wet periods. As grasses get older the amount of stem relative to the amount of leaf increases and overall forage quality decreases. Methods that promote the production of leaves over stems must therefore be used on grasslands managed for grazers. One example is fire, which as we have seen can stimulate the growth of new leaves.

Grasslands and grazers have evolved together for millennia, but grasses have not evolved as food sources for grazers. Grasses fight back against grazers, using anti-herbivore chemicals such as alkaloids, cyanide and phenols. Indole alkaloids make reed canary grass unpalatable and, in some cases, toxic to sheep. Cyanide-containing compounds can make sorghum leaves, but not the grains, lethal. Grassland dominated by highly palatable fescues and ryegrasses becomes highly toxic when infected with certain fungi.

Different grazers use landscapes in different ways and graze in different manners. Cattle use their tongues to pull up tufts of grass, leaving an uneven, tussocky sward. Dairy cattle are best raised on young grass, but beef cattle are more productive on mature grass. Sheep, like rabbits, nibble at grasses, producing a short sward, and avoid long grasses. Furthermore, trampling creates open areas, stimulating seed germination and plant colonization. However, overgrazing can change the fodder quality of grassland. In Britain the toxic plant common ragwort is of particular concern to the equestrian lobby, and its spread is a consequence of poor grazing management.

If livestock is to be fed over the lean months, grasses must be stored. Forage grasses can be stored either dry as hay or wet as silage. In both cases they must be harvested at their maximum nutritional value. As a method of preserving forage grasses, human cultures have practised haymaking for thousands of years. To produce the best hay the crop must be dried quickly and thoroughly before it is stooked or baled for storage. However, because haymaking can be highly weather dependent, over the past 30 years silage has become more popular in many Western European agricultural systems. Silage, pickled grass, is a major part of the winter diets of British livestock, and hundreds of thousands of hectares of grassland are converted into it each year. Silage is made by preserving grass in acidic conditions through fermentation with lactic acid bacteria; the same bacteria used to make foods such as sauerkraut and sourdough. Harvested grass is chopped up and heaped into a silage clamp, where as much air as possible is removed, then the whole pile is sealed with plastic. If air gets into the mix, silage spoils.

In some countries employing industrial livestock production, animals may never graze in fields but have rations made from cereals or concentrates manufactured from surprising sources. Epidemics such as 'mad cow disease' in the British cattle herd in the 1990s raise questions in some lobbies over the wisdom of divorcing grazers from the grasses with which they evolved.

Natural Grasslands as Forage

Europeans arriving in South Africa and North America were amazed at the quantity of grassland they encountered. Grasslands familiar to colonists from their homelands were tiny in comparison, and had been hard won by stripping land of forest. The hunter-gatherers and pastoralists who inhabited these grasslands had intimate knowledge of how to manage them and the animal populations they supported. Hunter-gatherers understand wild animal migration patterns; pastoralists understand the manipulation of patterns of grass growth. For example, animal herds may be moved up and down mountains or across plains as grasses grow through the changing seasons.

For a decade from 1652, Johan Anthoniszoon van Riebeeck sporadically chronicled how Dutch settlers and South Africa's indigenous Khoikhoi pastoralists used the plants and animals around the nascent settlement of Cape Town.[5] On 6 December 1652 he reported the migration of the indigenous Khoikhoi's flocks and herds, and that 'along the hill beside Table Mountain the country is covered with cattle and sheep as the grass', and within days there were 2,000 head 'within half a cannon shot of the Fort'.[6] Three years later, due to the annual migration the surrounding area was 'as full of cattle as grass in a field'.[7] The veld around Cape Town supported the pastoralists' migratory herds and the settlers' permanent herds. As well as acquiring their cattle and sheep stocks, the settlers learned to manage the veld from the Khoikhoi.[8] Traditionally, Khoikhoi pastoralists migrated with the spring grass so that their herds could take advantage of the new grass growth. When grasses became too rank, the Khoikhoi set fire to them, moved on and returned to the fresh green, rejuvenated veld after the rains.

By the end of the seventeenth century up to 7,000 cattle and about 50,000 sheep were grazing within 80 kilometres of Cape Town. Stock numbers increased ten-fold over the next century. Despite

William Blake's *The Shepherd*, from *Songs of Innocence* (*c.* 1795).

management, the veld started to show signs of becoming overgrazed; the shrubby rhinoceros bush began to invade.[9] As the settlers gradually expanded their grazing horizons, conflicts among settlers and between settlers and the indigenous pastoralists were inevitable. In the 1830s overgrazed grassland, combined with the effects of long-term drought, forced the migration of the Boers (descendents of Dutch settlers) towards the vast grasslands of the north and east of South Africa, away from political control by the British; the Great Trek was set in motion.[10] The migrants became known as the *voortrekkers*, and the consequences of this migration reverberated across the British Empire for the rest of the century.

Wool from merino sheep raised on the South African veld, the South American pampas and southern Australian grasslands became a major import into Victorian and Edwardian Britain. Sheep first become a mainstay of the English commercial and political life during the Middle Ages as the weavers of Flanders and Italy sought high-quality wool. By the fourteenth century wool was king. Today some of the elaborate buildings created through the wool trade are preserved in picturesque villages such as Lavenham in Suffolk. However, the need for highly productive pasture forced changes to traditional systems of land ownership and management.

Artificial Grasslands as Forage

The fourteenth-century wool economy was built on flourishing agricultural grasslands growing in the damp, mild British climate. British grasslands, which today cover approximately half of the islands' surface area, are virtually all products of human activities over the last five millennia. These grasslands are divided into three broad groups based on grazing quality: rough grazing, permanent pasture and rotational grassland (leys). About half of British grasslands comprise rough grazing, and are found in upland and marginal lowland areas. Rough grazing tends to be rich in grasses and other plants adapted to growing in low-nutrient conditions. As forage, however, rough grazing is suitable only for sheep and beef cattle, although even these need better grazing if they are being fattened for the spit. About 40 per cent of British grassland is permanent pasture, and most permanent pasture has been created through centuries of 'improvement' of lowland rough grazing by applications of fertilizers and land drainage. Permanent pasture must be fertilized regularly to maintain productivity. With careful grazing management systems, permanent pasture has become the mainstay of British livestock farming. Leys, which are resown every few years, comprise the remaining British grassland. Although they are expensive to establish they are extremely productive, if continually managed; once neglected leys revert to permanent pasture.

Nitrogen is the most common atmospheric gas and critical for plant growth. However, gaseous nitrogen is inert and bacteria must convert it into compounds plants can use. Unfortunately, nitrogen compounds are readily leached from soils. The supply of nitrogen therefore often limits plant growth, and to increase grass productivity it must be added to soil. As we have seen, natural grasslands contain many sorts of plants other than grasses. Notable, when considering the forage value of grasslands, are the legumes, many of which have nitrogen-fixing bacteria in their roots.

The power of muck to manipulate plant productivity was well known to classical writers. Practical experience, handed down from generation to generation, showed gardeners and farmers how to manipulate manure:

> who saveth in a paile, all the droppings of the houses, I mean the urine, and when the paile is full, spinckleth it on her Meadow, which causeth the grasse at first to look yellow, but after a little time, it growes wonderfully, that many of her [Kentish woman] neighbours wondered at it, and were like to accuse of her of witch-craft.[11]

By the mid-eighteenth century large-scale transformation of rough grassland to permanent pasture was under way. Land was being drained

James Sowerby's *Rye-grass*, 1796.

and fertilized with all manner of plant and animal waste products, including flesh and bones, bile, mucus, urine and ordure; organic matter for fertilizer was at a premium.

During the nineteenth century vast quantities of animal bones were imported from European slaughterhouses for the manufacture of bonemeal. More ghoulishly, the German chemist Justus von Liebig accused the British of converting the dead on European battlefields into plant food.[12] The discovery of industrial quantities of guano, the accumulated droppings of seabirds, led to a rich source of plant nutrients and profit for Victorian landowners and businessmen.

Fertilizer use changed completely in the twentieth century because of the Haber-Bosch process. Nitrogen was taken directly from the atmosphere and combined with hydrogen to produce ammonia, the raw material for industrial fertilizer manufacture. Bacteria were not needed to process atmospheric nitrogen; plant and animal waste did not have to be spread on fields. Nitrogen was no longer a limitation and the productivity of grasslands increased dramatically, but at an environmental cost.

When petrol and diesel made draught animals redundant, land was liberated from the production of fodder for transport and haulage.

Dung from grazing animals is fuel and fertilizer in rural economies.

John Frederick Herring's *The Harvest*, 1857. Before the invention of the internal combustion engine, animals were the major agricultural power source.

After the Second World War towns, cities and roads expanded into meadows and leys. Short-term economic realities led to pastures being ploughed and hedgerows being grubbed up to make way for fields of wheat. As agricultural production intensified, rough grassland (including flower-rich hay meadows) declined in the British countryside.[13] Grassland species evolved in conditions of low fertility. Once grasslands were covered with fertilizer many species could no longer compete with the few grasses that could make use of highly fertile conditions. In Britain grasslands with the lowest nitrogen input have more than twice as many plant species as grasslands with the highest nitrogen input.[14] On average, one plant species will disappear from each hectare of British and American grassland dressed with 2.5 kilograms of nitrogen. Potentially more worrying for those concerned with the restoration of flower-rich meadows is the discovery that the legacy of fertilizers persists in the soil for decades.[15]

Making Forage Better

Users of grassland have modified grassland landscapes for thousands of years in response to the needs of their animals. As the unidentified landowner quoted by Flint makes clear, the trick to making a living from grazing animals is to find (or grow) the right forage (usually a grass) in the right place, and manage the land in the right way. Traditionally, people had discovered valuable fodder grasses and how to manage them through trial and error.

During the nineteenth century enthusiastic European landowners started systematic searches for new fodder grasses, and began to conduct experiments with the aim of maximizing fodder productivity. The agricultural experiments conducted by the sixth Duke of Bedford's staff at Woburn Abbey were described in the popular book *Hortus Gramineus Woburnensis*. The book's subtitle, *An account of the results of experiments in the produce and nutritive qualities of different grasses and other plants used as the food of the more valuable domestic animals*, made the Duke's aims clear. In 1856 the British businessman John Bennet Lawes established a trial

William Ashford's *Landscape with Haymakers and a Distant View of a Georgian House*, c. 1780.

site at his ancestral home to study the effects of fertilizer treatments on grassland productivity. Lawes's home evolved into an agricultural research institute. His experiment, the Park Grass Experiment, is one of the oldest continuous ecological experiments in modern science.[16]

Lawes modified the environment in which fodder grasses grew but, as we have seen, the response of a grass to the environment is affected by its genetic make-up. When rough grazing in Britain is heavily fertilized, two grasses dominate the permanent pastures produced, perennial ryegrass and crested dog's-tail. In the early twentieth century, under the direction of the forage grass breeder George Stapledon, scientists at the Welsh Plant Breeding Institute selected strains of perennial ryegrass from across its geographical and ecological range adapted to many different climatic and trampling conditions. Today perennial ryegrass is one of the premier forage and amenity grasses.

Smooth meadow-grass is a highly variable species with many different chromosomes races. Some of these races accidentally crossed the Atlantic Ocean with early European settlers, who valued it as a fodder species. The species competed well with native American grasses and genotypes adapted to the new conditions flourished. Eventually, as the settlers moved, vast areas of prairie were colonized. Those strains selected in American soils transformed the prairies and became known as the legendary Kentucky bluegrass. True to the adage that grass is always greener on the other side, American Kentucky bluegrass was imported back to Europe to improve smooth meadow-grass as forage and turf.

Once good forage grass species have been found, the principles for improving their qualities are the same as those for improving cereals. The differences are the selection pressures. Flowers are the focus in cereals; foliage is the focus in forage.

ten

Making a Future

Mat-grass [marram] is one of those ordinations of nature, the
immediate use of which we are permitted to know, and whose
virtues are within our level of comprehension: . . . it stems the
torrent of an inundation of drifting sand.

JOHN LEONARD KNAPP, *Gramina Britannica* (1804)

The future is about the objects we create and the cultures we
build around us. Culturally and politically, grasses have a
unique position in the lives of humans. In Chinese culture
the grass bamboo, one of the Four Gentlemen, is thought to show
the virtues of a gentleman: tenacity, integrity and elegance. From the
Chinese Han Dynasty (206 BC–AD 220), ideas and information
have been transmitted within and across generations on bamboo
strips or on paper made from bamboo.[1] Grasses such as bamboo and
reed are used to make music, and all the major world religions use
grasses and grass products as metaphors. A grass (wheat) has come to
symbolize the ideals of the United Nations Food and Agriculture
Organization.

Ecologically, continental interiors have been shaped by the evolution of grasslands, while coastal grasses defend land from the
ravages of the sea. This century humans face major, long-term challenges, including how to feed an ever-increasing population and
how to respond to long-term environmental change. Despite these
long-term challenges having been high on global political agendas in

the last two decades, they now appear to have been surpassed by more immediate, short-term concerns; the crutch of technology is supporting indifference.

Transformation and Change

We have transformed natural landscapes to accommodate our farms, our cities and our channels of communication. Watercourses have been rerouted and polluted. Forests have been razed to the ground; trees have been replaced by domesticated grasses. Marshes and fenlands have been drained; sedges and rushes have been replaced by domesticated grasses. Savannahs and prairies have been ploughed; wild grasses have been replaced by domesticated grasses. However, high-intensity agriculture was not an invention of the Green Revolution; it has been practised for centuries. The sinuous terracing of mountainsides in the Andes, China and Southeast Asia is among the great human engineering feats over the last two millennia. Generations of farming communities made the terraces to trap soil and nutrients so crop yields could be maximized.

In addition to landscape transformation we have changed the world's climate. For most of our history we have not understood the impact that we have on the planet's climate. That has changed in the last two decades. The Earth's temperature is determined by the balance between heat gained from the sun and heat lost into space. Greenhouse gases such as carbon dioxide and methane provide a barrier to heat loss and are crucial to all life on Earth. As atmospheric greenhouse gas levels rise, the planet's surface temperature rises. One of these gases, carbon dioxide, is removed by plants, through the process of photosynthesis, in forms that cannot affect the atmosphere. Only when organisms decay and respire do they release carbon dioxide back into the atmosphere as part of the carbon cycle. Over about 350 million years, plants and marine organisms were crushed beneath ocean sediments to form fossil fuels such as coal, gas and oil,

Giant reed is used for building, as a garden plant and to make the reeds of clarinets.

trapping vast amounts of carbon from prehistoric atmospheres. As the Industrial Revolution gathered pace in the nineteenth century, large-scale consumption of fossil fuels started to take place. The carbon was released into the atmosphere, increasing overall greenhouse gas concentration.

Predictions about future climate change are, of course, uncertain and based on the outcomes of climate models. However, mean global surface temperature is expected to rise between 1 and 6°c by 2100. The global consequences of this are likely to be increased flood severity, droughts and extreme weather events. Global warming will exacerbate species extinctions as people move into ever-more marginal habitats, the environments traditionally given over to conservation. Extinctions per se are part of evolution; life on Earth will adapt to the changed conditions, as it has done through past mass extinctions. Our real concerns about global warming are how they will affect our lives, and whether we will be able to live comfortably in the changed conditions; some people may even be concerned about their grandchildren. More than a billion people could be displaced as sea levels rise by up to 60 centimetres. Billions of people may face extreme water shortages and hunger, leading to increased mass human migrations and war. Grasses might help us to mitigate or adapt to some environmental changes, as they have done in the past, but ultimately the issues are political rather than biological. With a finite amount of land, four issues will compete for our attention: land for living, land for food, land for fuel and land for conserving wild grasses and other organisms.

Grasses as Terraformers

The English naturalist John Leonard Knapp considered the sand-dune grass marram to be a divinely created terraformer. The abilities of marram to stabilize sand dunes are impressive. Since 1812 on average nearly 5 metres of land has been added annually to the dunes of Tentsmuir, near St Andrews, in Scotland.[2] Consequently, as you walk away from the sea through this dune system, you are walking through time – an ecological succession. The ocean of silvery-green grass rippling around you is marram. It is well adapted to life on sand dunes, where environmental stresses include high salinity and diurnal temperatures, persistent wind and high disturbance. The leaves are covered in a thick, waterproof layer (cuticle), and when temperatures or wind speeds increase the leaves roll up, protecting the plant from excessive water loss.[3]

Marram, one of the tunnelling perennial grasses, has a rhizome that is like a tough, living mesh holding heaps of sand in place. If the buds on the rhizomes remain in the dark, covered by sand, more marram rhizome is produced. If the rhizome buds are exposed to light they develop into leafy shoots, which eventually produce flowers. Marram interferes with wind movement, so that

Marram grass stabilizing sand dunes at Freshwater West, Pembrokeshire.

when wind-blown sand grains hit marram leaves they fall to the ground and accumulate around the plant base but the leaves continue to grow. The mobility of the soil surface is reduced and dune soils stabilize, letting other plants colonize, further modifying the newly created habitats. Over time, depending on environmental conditions, vast dune systems may develop. In Alaska, during the Pleistocene, a dune system some 7,000 square kilometres in extent formed, the remnants of which are visible today.[4] The importance of marram as a coastal defence has been recognized for centuries. In 1584 the English queen Elizabeth I decreed uprooting marram to be illegal. By the late seventeenth century Scottish monarchs extended these laws to the Scottish coast, and in 1741 it became a criminal offence to harvest or possess marram within 8 miles of the British coast.[5]

Marram is one of several botanical civil engineers whose attributes have been exploited by human engineers and conservationists to stabilize labile environments. Other grasses used as ecosystem engineers include cord-grasses on mudflats and salt marshes, and reeds on lake and river margins.

The erosion of soil through the combined actions of water, wind and cultivation is extensive. Erosion may have dramatic effects on the lives of humans.[6] In the 1990s the consequences of Chinese hillsides, stripped of their forests, slipping into the Yangtze River were devastating for tens of thousands of Chinese peasants. About one-third of the planet's land area has been converted to agriculture, although in the past 40 years, approximately one-third of this agricultural land has had to be abandoned because of soil erosion. Fertilizers derived from fossil fuels provide a temporary fix to enhance the fertility of eroded soils. The final decades of the twentieth century were marked by the razing of the Amazonian rainforest to create cattle pasture, producing iconic images of environmental mismanagement.

Any plant is technically capable of preventing the erosion of soil on land stripped of native vegetation. However, grasses are particularly effective since many species naturally grow gregariously and develop rapidly. Annual grasses achieve the feat by sheer force of numbers. Perennial grasses that creep over the soil surface prevent soil movement, while tunnelling grasses bind soil particles with their rhizomes and roots. However, some grasses not only stabilize soils, but have the capacity to increase soil fertility over time. In North America native switchgrass has been promoted as an agent of soil conservation and amelioration in areas of the Corn Belt formerly covered by prairie, together with roadsides and river margins. The grass protects the soil against wind and water erosion, but the deep roots increase soil fertility, permeability and humus levels, returning prairie soils that have been degraded by cereal production to their former quality.

The idea of using grasses as biological scrubbers to clean polluted habitats is both culturally potent and evocative. In the 1950s grasses helped researchers study adaption to metal-populated sites and demonstrated Darwin's ideas of evolution in action, but also promised to clean up the soil heaps and polluted sites left behind by industry. However, when these grasses were tested in field conditions they failed to live up to the promise, although this has not stopped the search for other metal-scrubbing grasses. Whether Napier grass lives up to expectations is a matter for the future.[7] One grass that has proven to be an effective scrubber is common reed in the treatment of waste water (for example effluent from homes and farms). Water separated from solid matter trickles through artificial wetlands, and bacteria on the surfaces of the roots remove nutrients from the water so that clean water may be released to natural water courses.[8]

Grasses as Biofuels

As a result of concerns about carbon emissions, declining fossil fuel supplies and high fuel prices, energy is a major societal issue. Today most fuels are directly or indirectly derived from energy reserves produced by prehistoric photosynthesis. Biofuels, energy sources derived from present-day photosynthesis, have become a modern mantra for a sustainable future. Most human history has been fuelled by brute force of human and animal labour, and solid bio-fuels (biomass) such as wood or dried faeces. In addition to biomass, modern biofuels include liquid fuels such as alcohol, and gases such as methane. In 2011 the International Energy Agency estimated that biofuels could meet about a quarter of transportation fuel needs by 2050.[9]

Globally ethanol, produced by fermentation of sugars and starches, is the most commonly produced and used liquid biofuel, especially in sugar-rich Brazil. The Brazilian ethanol economy was born during the oil crisis of the 1970s and has been pursued by successive governments. Today ethanol accounts for about 40 per cent of all liquid fuel used in Brazil.[10] The most common grasses used in ethanol manufacture are sugar cane and maize. Cellulose-rich grasses, such as switchgrass and miscanthus, are grown as biomass for energy production. However, the waste products (clinker) produced when grasses, with their high silica contents, are burned can cause problems in industrial processes.[11] Second-generation biofuels use chemicals and enzymes to convert cellulose in grass-cell walls into liquid fuels efficiently.[12] Fungi and

Alcohol, derived from sugar cane, is a major fuel in Brazil and is available at every petrol station.

Native tropical forest on the Atlantic coast of Brazil is cleared
for grassland dominated by introduced grasses.

bacteria are particularly effective at breaking down complex cellulose
molecules into simple substances that can be used for ethanol synthesis. The production of ethanol from cellulose is technically complex,
although a model is found in nature: in the guts of ruminant grazers
such as cattle and camels. Cattle are mobile cellulose-fermentation
tanks. Fed by grass, the intestinal bacteria of cattle produce sugars and
methane, leaving a residue of unprocessed material (faeces). As water
is lost, a cowpat matures through stages from chocolate mousse
through crème brûlée to biscuit. Methane from cows cannot be captured, but their faeces can be used as either a fuel or a soil additive to
improve texture and fertility. Consequently, in some societies burning
faeces as a biofuel will limit agricultural productivity, since manure may
be the only source of fertilizer available.

The economics and ethics of biofuel production are topics of great debate and detailed analysis.[13] Understanding biofuel economics is complicated by both government subsidies and the difficulties of determining net energy gain. There are diverse routes by which energy, usually from fossil fuels, is consumed to transform a field of grass into a forecourt product. Energy is consumed in planting, cultivating, irrigating and harvesting the crop, protecting it from pests and diseases, transporting it to the production plant, processing, fermenting, distilling and drying the biofuel, and transporting the biofuel to retail outlets. Some of these energy needs may be offset by burning waste products, such as sugar-cane waste (bagasse) in the distillation of cane-derived ethanol. The use of food cereals such as maize, wheat and barley as biofuel feedstocks has also exposed biofuel ventures to ethical charges associated with using food to produce fuel, leading to world food-price distortion. Growing fuels has implications for habitat transformation; land is converted from food to fuel production or habitats are destroyed to grow fuel. The issues are complex and will involve us in choices, since land area is limited. Do we want to use limited land for food, fuel, cities or conservation?

Grasses in Construction

The giant Southeast Asian timber bamboos can reach 30 metres in height and are obvious grasses to use in constructing our world. The silica-rich walls of bamboo cells are impregnated with tiny, flint-like fragments that make intact stems very tough and split stems very sharp. Furthermore, bamboo stems resist forces of compression, tension and torsion, but are easily split, woven, twisted and bent. For construction, bamboo stems must be harvested when they are at their greatest strength and lowest sugar content. Furthermore, bamboo quality depends on how bamboo is raised in the field, how it is harvested and processed, and how the final products are maintained. Bamboo stems, bent and lashed, form the bases of traditional architecture in South and East Asia and the South Pacific, whilst twisted bamboo stems have been used to make cables for suspension bridges. Bamboo strips, planed, cleaned and dried, can be glued together to make hard-wearing laminates for flooring, carpentry and cabinet making.

Large bamboo stems make excellent pipes for moving water, if the walls dividing the stems at the nodes are broken. If the walls are left intact and sections cut, excellent cooking pots are produced; bamboo pots are both fireproof and waterproof. In 1837, on one cold morning in the Organ Mountains of Brazil, the explorer George Gardner was grateful for the breakfast that had been cooked in pots made from the stem of a giant bamboo. However, he found the water that accumulated in bamboo stems 'noisome', even in extremis, despite the praise heaped upon it by other travellers.[14] Besides water, concretions of silica (bamboo manna, *tawashir*), also found inside bamboo stems, have attracted the attention of physicians and the curious for thousands of years.[15]

The adaptability of bamboo as a construction material, its image as a natural product and its association with Eastern cultures has lent

Adlard's engraving *Vegetation of Bamboos in Java*, 1874, showing bamboo being used for bridge construction.

tremendous cachet to this grass in the minds of Western consumers. Bamboo fibres are very short and have been used for centuries in paper manufacture. During the last century it was discovered that the cellulose in bamboo fibres could be transformed into a synthetic fibre, rayon, which could be spun into a yarn for textile manufacture. To produce rayon, bamboo stems are dissolved in a chemical cocktail, but despite the industrial processes involved, the ecological image of the grass has led some business people to market rayon as a 'natural' bamboo fabric.

Bamboo is an obvious construction grass. However, dried thatching grasses such as common reed, and living turf grasses that protect the roofs of traditional houses in Iceland, are important for keeping the elements at bay. Just as genetic modification of cereals promises to herald major changes as genes are moved across previously impossible barriers, so some grasses may be capable of synthesizing chemical building blocks of the future. For example, a genetically modified switchgrass has been produced that is capable of accumulating 3.7 per cent of its dry weight as the plastic polymer polyhydroxybutyrate.[16]

eleven

Playing the Field

The grass was green above the dead boy's grave, and trodden by feet so small and light, that not a daisy drooped its head beneath their pressure.

CHARLES DICKENS, *The Life and Adventures of Nicholas Nickleby* (1838–9)

An apocryphal story relates how a tourist admired an Oxbridge college lawn so much that he asked the groundsman how he could grow one like it. The groundsman replied that he would need to scarify, prick, roll, fertilize and mow it – for 300 years. Besides the groundsman having a fancy for hyperbole, the anecdote emphasizes that producing a first-class lawn requires time, effort and money. However, the production of a green sward for leisure is not just about the effort of husbandry; the right selection of grasses must be made. Grasses suitable for the delicate steps of an Oxbridge don are very different from those suitable for a garden where children play. The grasses upon which multimillion-pound ball games are played, a surface that rarely merits mention until a team loses and a scapegoat is needed, are different from those for an urban park. Furthermore, different games require different grass mixes. Yet the environmental damage done by lawns and playing surfaces is not to be underestimated. Bright green golf courses in desert landscapes, artificially maintained by transporting vast amounts of scarce water through parched lands, are an abomination. Despite

overleaf: A typical British multi-purpose, suburban lawn.

the differences among natural grasslands and cultivated swards, the adaptations shown by wild grasses are precisely those needed for grasses to succeed in lawns; lawnmowers are no more than mechanical grazers.

Lawns in Landscapes

The lawn is a familiar and powerful British cultural stereotype. The damp maritime climate of Western Europe is ideal for lawn cultivation – unlike many of parts of the empire to which the British tried to export lawn culture and the public school games played upon it. Goscinny and Uderzo's *Asterix in Britain* (1970) had a minor character pushed beyond endurance by a Roman cohort about to trample his lawn. The stereotype of the English village green and cricket even became part of the 2012 Olympics opening ceremony.

Lawns appear to have begun as animal enclosures in medieval Europe. By the sixteenth century they were part of garden landscapes and had come to mean an area of closely mown or grazed grass. However, it was not until the mid-nineteenth century that lawns became commonplace. Forty years ago it was estimated that about 1.5 per cent of the land area of the United Kingdom was covered with recreational grassland (lawns and sports fields).[1] In 2005 a similar

Paul Sandby's *North West View of Wakefield Lodge in Whittlebury Forest, Northamptonshire*, 1767, showing the setting created by Capability Brown.

School playing field.

percentage of the United States was estimated to be covered with recreational grassland.

Symbolically, lawns are used to assert political and social order, power over nature, wealth and suburban uniformity. The landscape designer Capability Brown used the lawn to assert a landowner's power. His clients could afford to set aside large areas of land for non-productive purposes and pay a workforce to look after it.[2] Lawn maintenance was time consuming and required people to trim the grass with scythes or animals to graze it. When the rotary lawnmower was invented in the 1820s, lawns could be maintained more easily and the turf cropped more closely than with a scythe, without the inconvenience of a peppering of animal faeces. As lawn maintenance became simpler and people became wealthier, the middle classes of nineteenth-century Britain could aspire to own a lawn, and municipal parks and sports fields became practical, readily maintained possibilities. Ritual and culture bordering on the obsessive developed around the lawn, with commerce feeding an appetite for all manner of devices for lawn primping and fetishization.

However, over the last century there have been times when expanses of public and private recreational grass have been politically unacceptable. Part of the British Dig for Victory Campaign of the Second World War emphasized that unproductive lawns could be transformed to productive land.[3] Following the economic follies of the late twentieth and early twenty-first centuries, the Obamas reprised this campaign in the United States by ordering a token patch of grass in the Whitehouse grounds to be given over to vegetable growing.[4] In the UK the politics and economics of recreational grasslands are stark. Cash-strapped schools and local authorities may have extensive recreational grasslands in highly desirable areas. Selling playing fields for short-term economic gain may be too much of a temptation when compared with their long-term amenity value.[5]

Making Recreational Grassland

Unlike pasture grasses where nutritional qualities are important, ideal recreational grasses must persist when closely and frequently mown, have low growth, be tolerant of heavy wear and look good all year around. Only a handful of grass species meet these exacting demands. Grasses such as fescues and bents are tolerant of close mowing (to about 5 millimetres) and produce a fine, tight sward, but grow poorly when heavily trampled. In contrast, species such as perennial ryegrass tolerate heavy wear but not close mowing. As Western Europeans started to settle in the tropics and subtropics they tried to recreate their recreational landscapes using grasses imported from Western Europe. However, they soon discovered that to create passable lawns and playing surfaces they had to plant C_4 grasses such as St Augustine grass, Bermuda grass and kikuyu grass, rather than the C_3 grasses with which they were familiar.

To make a lawn grass plants must be multiplied by sexual propagation, using seed, or by clonal propagation, using some form of cutting. Seeds are usually genetically distinct from their parents and are mobile, self-contained packets that tolerate desiccation and germinate in response to environmental conditions. Clonal propagation relies on any living plant cell being able to regenerate into any other plant cell (totipotency). Anyone who has broken a leaf or a stem from a desired plant, pushed it into soil and seen a new plant regenerate is familiar with the process. In Western Europe seeding a prepared surface usually produces a lawn quickly and easily. In the tropics lawns are formed by sodding, which relies on vegetative propagation. Fragments of stolon or rhizome are pushed into mud, start to grow and eventually creep or tunnel to form a continuous sward. In contrast, turfing is like grafting skin – grass is carefully stripped from one area and rolled out over another, and the roots eventually anchor the turf in place. Consequently, land must be set aside to produce seed, sod and turf for recreational grasses.

Turf and Turf Management

Much science, plant breeding and generations of practical trial and error have gone into determining the mixtures necessary for the multiple uses to which recreational grasslands are put. However, there is often a more emotional reaction when plants other than grasses are found in recreational grasslands; daisies and dandelions are weeds, whilst mosses are evidence of neglect. Getting the best out of recreational grassland requires selecting the right grasses, preparing the planting areas and actively maintaining them.

There are three types of lawn: general purpose, shady and fine. A grass mix for a general-purpose lawn might include Highland bent, red fescue, dwarf cultivars of perennial ryegrass and smooth meadow grass. The narrow leaves of the bent and fescue ensure that the turf has a fine structure, whilst the deep roots or well-developed rhizomes of the other species aid in their resistance to wear. Shady situations present some of the most difficult conditions in which to establish lawns; grassland species are not well adapted to woodlands and woodland grasses do not make good lawns. Inclusion of rough meadow-grass, one of the most adaptable of temperate grasses, into a mix of bent and fescue is often effective in shady areas. In the case of fine lawns, mixtures of bents (especially common

Unknown artist, *A Game of Cricket*, c. 1790–99.

and Highland) and fescues (especially red and Chewing's) will produce a slow-growing sward that can be closely mown. Although such lawns are aesthetically appealing they are not particularly tolerant of heavy use.

The species used in turf for sports fields, courses, greens and pitches are similar to those used in lawns. However, as a consequence of the economic importance of professional and semi-professional games, considerable investment and research has gone into selecting and breeding cultivars of familiar grasses. Ideal conditions for sport may not be ideal for the grass growth. Surfaces are in constant danger of being churned up by stud-footed rugby and football players hurtling around a pitch week after week, whilst closely mown golfing and bowling greens are in danger of suffering the effects of overgrazing. The methods used by recreational grass breeders are the same as those of food grass breeders. The genetic variation across the ecological and geographical range of natural populations of recreational grasses is the starting point for breeding. Rather than selecting for

Spencer Gore's *Tennis at Hertingfordbury*, 1910.

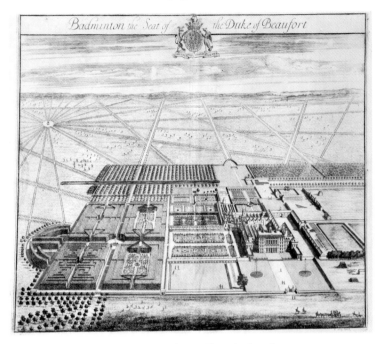

Johannes Kip, Badminton, the Seat of the Duke of Beaufort, c. 1724.

grain size and number, recreational grass breeders might be more concerned with rooting density and ability to recover from mechanical damage, although both groups of breeders are concerned with disease resistance. Consequently, there are dozens of grass cultivars for use in particular situations on sports surfaces.

Sports surfaces are not uniform; they suffer different amounts of use and abuse. Golf courses comprise close-mown tees and greens, and less tended fairways and roughs. On a cricket pitch, the wicket might be planted with dwarf cultivars of perennial ryegrass for durability and cultivars of bent and fescue for a close-mown surface, whilst the outfield might comprise bents and fescues that bind the surface but do not need to be mown with the same frequency as swards containing ryegrass. Wherever recreational grasslands are found they are dynamic, living systems capable of acclimatizing to local conditions. In a grass mix, ryegrass will predominate in the heavily used areas, whilst bent and fescue will predominate in less heavily used areas. Moreover, in the better drained areas fescue is likely to dominate over bent.

First-class recreational turf production requires intensive horticulture, including high fertilizer applications, heavy watering and extensive mowing. In the U.S. it has been estimated that the watering of recreational grass accounts for approximately 75 per cent of total household water use. Consequently efforts are being made to breed grass cultivars that thrive on low water and fertilizer input. On a more positive side, computer models in the United States show that recreational grassland has the potential to lock up atmospheric carbon in forms that will not contribute to global warming. Ironically, to do this effectively grasslands must be heavily managed; they need frequent water and nitrogen inputs.[6]

Compared with pastures or natural grasslands, few species (even grasses) are found in recreational grassland. However, earthworms are commonly found. Charles Darwin had no doubts about the importance of earthworms for grassland health:

> when we behold a wide, turf-covered expanse, we should remember that its smoothness, on which so much of its beauty depends, is mainly due to all the inequalities having been slowly levelled by worms. It is a marvellous reflection that the whole of the superficial mould over any such expanse has passed, and will again pass, every few years through the bodies of worms. The plough is one of the most ancient and most valuable of man's inventions; but long before he existed the land was in fact regularly ploughed, and still continues to be thus ploughed by earth-worms. It may be doubted whether there are many other animals which have played so important a part in the history of the world.[7]

In contrast, worm casts left behind as soil passes though earthworms' digestive tracts produce horrified reactions in some vermiphobe lawn owners and groundsmen. Worm casts are blamed for everything from making grass surfaces unsightly and slippery, to upsetting sports, ruining lawnmowers, providing opportunities for weed invasions and attracting pests such as birds and moles. No amount of biological argument will deter the turf obsessive from trying to eliminate earthworms by raising soil acidity and physically extracting or killing them, using arsenals of often restricted use chemicals. Perhaps the greatest boon for such people is the spread of the New Zealand flatworm, with its almost exclusive diet of earthworms. Since accidental introduction of the flatworm to Ireland in the early 1960s, it has spread to the cooler parts of northern Britain and continental Europe. However, another side of British earthworm eccentricity is found in the annual earthworm charming championship held at Willaston in Cheshire, where people compete to collect the most earthworms from a fixed area of turf in a fixed time.

twelve

Tramping the World

ᚼᚼᚼ

The hills around the Cidade do Serro are covered with a grass which the Brazilians called Capim gordura . . . It is covered with an oily viscous matter, and universally makes its appearance in those tracts, which have been cleared of virgin forest for the purposes of cultivation; both cattle and horses are very fond of it, but although they are soon fattened on it, the latter get short-winded, if they feed on it for any length of time.

GEORGE GARDNER, *Travels in the Interior of Brazil* (1846)

I n Europe before the mid-seventeenth century, weeds were widely believed to be produced spontaneously from soil. Pliny the Elder went further, taking the ancient belief that useful grasses, such as wheat and barley, could be transformed into apparently useless grasses, such as oats:

the first of all forms of disease in wheat is the oat. Barley also degenerates into oats, in such a way that the oat itself counts as a kind of corn . . . The degeneration in question is principally due to dampness of soil and climate, but a subsidiary cause is contained in weakness of the seed, if it is held back too long in the ground before it shoots out.[1]

Such accounts reveal that people were unaware seeds could lie dormant in the soil for decades before germinating. However, stories of wheat and barley grains germinating after thousands of years locked away in Egyptian tombs are probably apocryphal.

In addition to travelling in time, grasses respond to their environments by travelling in space. They expand their ranges when conditions are good, and contract them when conditions are poor. The common reed was one of the first plants reported from Krakatau after the Indonesian volcano exploded in 1883.[2] Humans have extended the ranges of some grasses far beyond that which could be achieved by natural dispersal. Under the pampering hand of humans, the major food grasses have moved out of their cradles of origin to colonize vast continental areas. Other grasses have been moved accidentally, taking full advantage of opportunities offered by new environments.

In 1840 the Scottish botanist and Brazilian explorer George Gardner left Serro, in the state of Minas Gerais. He was making his way back to Rio de Janeiro, having spent two years travelling thousands of miles through central Brazil collecting plants. Gardner noticed that the hills were covered with *capim gordura*, or molasses grass, a particularly sticky, linseed-scented grass, and a favourite food of the cattle and horses that fed the Brazilian population and powered her internal transportation network. Eventually Gardner became tired of seeing the grass as he witnessed the beginning of the wholesale destruction of the Brazilian Atlantic forest for coffee production. He predicted that extensive tracts of central Brazil would become covered by *capim gordura* as land was stripped of its native forest and savannah.

Capim gordura was first described in 1812 by the Frenchman Palisot de Beauvois, based on a specimen given to him by the French botanist Antoine de Jussieu, which had been collected in Rio de Janeiro. Botanical dogma of the time held that the grass was native to Brazil. However, Gardner argued that *capim gordura* was introduced to Brazil and moved around by the sticky spikelets which adhered to horse troops and cattle droves.[3] We now know that *capim gordura* is native to Africa. Another African grass first described from specimens collected in Brazil is *jaraguá*. It is tempting to conjecture that these grasses, which today choke parts of central Brazil, were transported from

4393.

Melinis minutiflora h. cu. b

Nᵒ 4393 *Gardner*
Goyaz.

Specimen of *capím gordura* collected in Goiás, Brazil by George Gardner in 1840.

Africa with the slaves that were the bedrock of colonial Brazilian economics; more 'gifts' from Africa to the Americas.

Weed or Crop?

Grasses are useful as crops, but the close relatives of these crops may be destructive as weeds. The duality is reflected in the difficulty of defining a crop and a weed. In traditional field systems crops and weeds often live side by side. Crop relatives may even be weedy, growing amongst the crop itself, and exchanging genes so that subsequent generations of planted grains will be crop-weed hybrids. Consequently, these systems are highly dynamic, full of diverse individuals that are well adapted to local conditions. These plants are called landraces, and are extremely important genetic reservoirs for disease-resistance genes used in modern crop breeding. The ability of crops and weeds to intergrade is a concern for those interested in growing herbicide-resistant crops and those worried about the formation of herbicide-resistant weeds.[4] In the United States a study of pollen movement among herbicide-tolerant creeping bent and its wild relatives was conducted.[5] It found that during one season the majority of genes moved less than 2 kilometres, with limited gene movement up to 21 kilometres. Three years after the herbicide-resistant bent had been removed, 62 per cent of bent plants still contained the herbicide-tolerance gene. In this particular case, the herbicide-tolerance gene persisted among the weedy plants.

The word crop typically refers to a plant grown for the purpose of later harvest. Importantly, this includes grasses deliberately planted and genetically altered (or domesticated) and wild grasses merely cosseted by human activities (or cultivated). Weed definitions are broader than crop definitions, ranging from 'a plant whose virtues have not yet been discovered', through 'a plant out of place, or growing where it is not wanted', to simply 'an unwanted plant'.[6] Such definitions underline visceral human responses to particular plants. More objective and useful definitions account for plant ecology, including 'opportunistic species that follow human disturbance of the habitat' and 'a plant which contests with man for the possession of the soil'.[7]

Annual meadow grass is a small European grass that is native to Britain and commonly found as a weed of anthropogenic situations. In North America it is a common weed of grass swards that is of particular concern on golf courses, although green managers display the full range of opinions about this grass. For some, annual meadow grass is loathsome and must be controlled at all cost – they even go so far as to make golfers put new spikes on their shoes before 'spoiling a good walk'. Other green keepers are more resigned, taking the view that since the grass is so successful, strains suitable for golf courses should be encouraged.[8] Another of the world's worst weeds, common reed, is also one of the most useful non-cereal grasses, as it is an important wildlife habitat, an important building material and a valuable water purifier.

Ecologically, characteristics that make grasses important arable or pasture crops also make them effective colonizers. They have short life cycles, and are good at getting around and exploiting disturbed areas. They may produce large amounts of seed, often by having sex with themselves. They may fragment their own bodies, forming natural monocultures. Some wild grasses even mimic the cereal crops they infest, making them very difficult to remove. Grasses are botanical camp followers, opportunists capable of colonizing the habitats created by humans and hitching lifts as humans or their animals move.

Taking Over

Most grasses outside their native ranges do not take hold on alien shores. Some of the immigrants, the adventives, take hold for a short period, then die out after a few generations. Others are more persistent – they become naturalized and behave like native species. Finally, a few naturalized species become prominent in their new homes; these vigorous and prolific invasives can cause enormous environmental and economic damage. It is impossible to tell what the fate of a particular grass will be if introduced just from looking at it. The best that one can do is look at probabilities. The Ten Rule states that for 100 species that are introduced, ten species will become naturalized and of these one will become invasive.[9]

Cheatgrass, or drooping brome, an annual Eurasian grass, is widely introduced outside its native range. In Britain it is merely a rare adventive, but in North America it is a very successful invasive grass covering vast areas of western North America. The grass was introduced, apparently multiple times, into North America in the late nineteenth century. By the first decade of the twentieth century cheatgrass was well established in a few localities, and by the Second World War it dominated at least 200,000 square kilometres of western North America; its present range.[10] This explosive expansion was summed up by Aldo Leopold: 'one simply woke up one fine spring to find the range dominated by a new weed.'[11] Leopold's statement emphasizes that invasive species are often only recognized once they reach such a density that they can no longer be overlooked; the invasive apparently appears everywhere but comes from nowhere. As a result, studies of how plants spread and become weeds are usually conducted retrospectively.

It is cheatgrass's biology that has made it a successful invader of scrub-steppe ecosystems in western North America.[12] Grains germinate with the autumn rain, so the young plants can take immediate advantage of the spring. Having deep roots, cheatgrass readily captures moisture and nutrients from the soil, outcompeting the seedlings of native perennial grasses. Cheatgrass produces large amounts of grain by self-fertilization, and the grains are dispersed by wind and animals. In the soil, grains remain viable for up to five years, although the dormancy of a proportion of the grains will be broken by high summer temperatures. In addition, cheatgrass is highly flammable and alters the fire dynamics of the ecosystems it invades. Fire is crucial for the ecological success of cheatgrass, creating sites that can be exploited by the grass. Consequently, cheatgrass readily transforms ecosystems dominated by perennial grasses into ecosystems dominated by annual grasses.

An inflorescence of wall barley embedded in a woolly jumper.

Dispersal of genes through pollination and seedling establishment is essential to give grasses good starts in life. Grasses may have spikelets covered in spines, hooks and elaborate awns, and bristles to help grains escape their parents and bury themselves in the soil. Some British children know the delight of throwing the dart-like ears of wall barley and seeing them stick to hair and clothes; these children have discovered that grass-dispersal mechanisms can be fun. However, to farmers this grass is no fun; the ears can penetrate the skins of livestock, which led one commentator to state that 'the eradication of this grass, or the cutting down before seed time, would be an act of mercy'.[13] Wall-barley awns are covered with microscopic barbs that trap the ears in fur and feathers – and clothing.

Many grasses make use of animal dispersal. Walking through Neotropical grasslands during the dry season, when grasses appear

Capim gordura invading native woodland in Serra da Moida, Goiás, Brazil.

like little more than straw, one becomes covered in grass fruits. Some of the most irritating are the hooked and spiked fruit clusters of bur grasses and the torpedo-like fruits of needle grasses. The latter are well named; they have hard, pointed tips surrounded by harpoon-like hairs, with long, twisted awns at the other end. The awns are hygroscopic; they twist and turn as humidity levels change, driving the fruits through trousers and into flesh, while the hairs around the tip prevent the fruits from being pulled out. These fruits are adapted for burial – for being drilled into sandy or broken soils.[14] The mechanism is called trypanocarpy, an apt description derived from the ancient practice of boring holes in skulls to release evil spirits. In this case, weeds may be the 'evil spirits' released by these grains. These grasses are merely nuisances to travellers, but to farmers areas dominated by such grasses become useless for fodder; the armed fruits embed themselves in the mouths and skins of grazing animals.

The multifarious means by which humans have aided the movement of grasses across the planet can be glimpsed by studying the alien grasses of the British Isles. Nearly 600 species of alien grass have been recorded in Britain, of which about 60 have become established.[15] In the early twentieth century British botanists became interested in accidental botanical immigrants and searched for new grasses in places where human movements were greatest, such as the docks in Liverpool, Bristol and London, and wool-processing factories in Tweedside. Many of the alien grasses appear to have come from South America, South Africa and Australia, trapped in raw sheep fleeces and mixed with poorly cleaned grain. Other important sources of alien grasses were hay, imported as animal fodder or used as packing materials, and esparto, the grasses used for making paper, ropes and sails. By the close of the century trade patterns and the types of goods traded had changed, and the most significant source of alien grasses had become bird seed. Social upheavals such as warfare and mass migrations also provide excellent opportunities for grasses to move, to experiment with new habitats and, potentially, to become weeds.

Gardeners and agriculturalists have been adept at moving grasses across the globe, particularly during the last century. Besides being used for lawns, exotic grasses are utilized in gardens and landscaping to provide texture, form and colour throughout the year in many different situations. Few of these grasses have yet become weeds, although some have the potential to do so. For example, there is evidence that the temperate South America pampas grass has become established outside gardens in Britain. Agriculturalists have deliberately introduced exotic grasses such as tussac-grass in the hope of increasing farmland productivity. In 1845 tussac-grass was introduced to the Shetlands from the Falkland Islands, with the enthusiastic endorsement of Joseph Hooker, the man who was destined to become the director of the Royal Botanic Gardens, Kew in the latter part of the nineteenth century.

The splendid *Tussack Grass* is the gold and the glory of the Falklands, and it will yet, I hope, make the fortune of Orkney

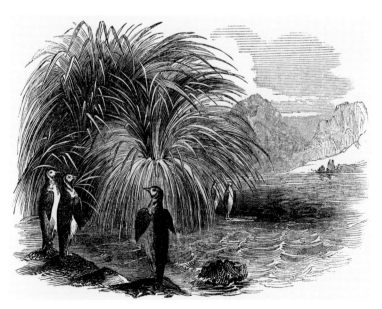

Tussac-grass depicted as an important shelter for penguins and 'seawolves' (sea lions) in the Falkland Islands by Joseph Hooker in 1843.

Birdseed is one of the main routes for accidental introduction of grasses in the UK.

and the owners of Irish peat-bogs. Every animal here devours this grass with avidity, and fattens upon it, in a short time . . . The blades are about six feet long, and from two to three hundred shoots spring from one plant. I have proved, by several experiments, that a man can cut one hundred bundles in a day, and a horse will greedily eat five of these bundles in that time. Indeed, so fond of it are both horses and cows, that they will devour dry *Tussack* thatch from the roofs of the cottages, in preference to good grass . . . It loves a rank, wet, peatbog, with the sea-spray dashing over it, and wherever the waves beat with the greatest vehemence, and the saline spray is carried farthest, there the *Tussack Grass* thrives the best, provided also it is on the soil it prefers.[16]

However, despite paeans of praise from many Victorian botanists, tussac-grass planting did not take off. After 170 years the grass has remained restricted to the few localities of its original introduction.[17] Despite having the potential to spread and become a weed, tussac-grass has not yet done so.

Feb.¹ 1 1803 Published by Ja.ˢ Sowerby London.

James Sowerby's *Bearded Darnel*, 1803.

Barnyard grasses overrun a wide variety of crops, including maize and rice, and often appear indistinguishable from the crops, especially at the vegetative stage; they are known as crop mimics. *Echinochloa oryzoides* is a rice mimic and obligate rice-field weed that has spread across Asia and many of the world's rice-growing regions. Because of the similarity between *E. oryzoides* and rice, weeding is difficult and many weed seedlings are overlooked. Weed grains are therefore harvested with the rice crop, and the weed is readily spread in the contaminated rice. For example, genetic data has shown that Australian *E. oryzoides* was derived from infected rice introduced from California just before the Second World War.[18]

Another famous crop mimic is darnel, the tares of the Bible This annual weedy grass used to be very common in European cereal fields; it remains common in the fields of the Near East. It also has the reputation for containing psychoactive toxins, which led to its association with the cults of Demeter and Persephone in Classical Greece.[19] In Middle Eastern medicine it was a painkiller and John Gerard reports that

> being drunke in sowre or harsh red Wine, [darnel] stoppeth the laske, and the ouermuch flowing of the flowers or menses, and is a remedie for those that pisse in bed.[20]

The toxicity of darnel grains appears to be due to a complex interaction involving fungi, nematodes and bacteria.[21] In the archaeological record darnel emerges at about the same time, and in the same region, as wheat and barley. The selection pressures on darnel were similar to those on barley and wheat, and darnel therefore shows many of the traits associated with the domestication syndrome of these cereals. As in the case of barnyard grasses, the reserve of darnel grains is not in the soil but in the grain harvest. Modern seed-cleaning techniques have reduced darnel infestations in developed countries, but infestations remain common in North Africa and Asia.

Globalization in the late twentieth century has become a cliché, but the opportunities for grasses to travel across continents to exploit habitats are now immense. We have seen that grasses can arrive accidentally, but deliberate movements of grasses are also of concern. New crop grasses are being studied and planted, an example being miscanthus for biofuel. In the garden or the field these grasses are unlikely to pose a risk. However, we do not know what will happen if they escape into the wild. The control of weedy grasses requires constant vigilance. In the United States and Europe, Italian ryegrass is starting to become a successful weed of winter wheat, apparently though mimicry.

We have been supported by grasses throughout our evolutionary history. Unconscious decisions made by farmers 400 generations ago affect our food choices today. With more information about the grasses around us, we can no longer claim ignorance about the importance of grasses in our lives. Over the next 50 years we face the challenge of maintaining food, water and energy supplies for a remorselessly expanding, ageing human population. Plants must be at the centre of our solutions to these challenges, and we must use what we have learned about grass biology to bend them once more to our desires.

Appendix: Scientific Names

❧❧❧

The scientific names of the species mentioned by their common names in the main text are given here. Family names for plants and fungi that are not members of the Poaceae are given in parentheses after the scientific names.

African rice	*Oryza glaberrima*
Annual meadow grass	*Poa annua*
Antarctic hairgrass	*Deschampsia antarctica*
Arrow grass	*Gynerium sagittatum*
Asian rice	*Oryza sativa*
Bamboo	Poaceae, subfamily Bambusoideae generally or tribe Bambuseae specifically
Barberry	*Berberis vulgaris* (Berberidaceae)
Barley	*Hordeum* spp.
Barley, cultivated	*Hordeum vulgare*
Barnyard grass	*Echinochloa* spp.
Barnyard millet	*Echinochloa frumentacea*
Bearded darnel	*Lolium temulentum*
Bent	*Agrostis* spp.
Bermuda grass	*Cynodon dactylon*
Big bluestem	*Andropogon furcatus*
Blue grass	*Poa pratensis*
Bread wheat	*Triticum aestivum* ssp. *aestivum*
Bristle sedge	*Carex microglochin* (Cyperaceae)
Broomrape	*Orobanche* spp. (Orobanchaceae)
Buffalo grass	*Buchloë dactyloides*
Bur grass	*Cenchrus* spp.
Bur-reed	*Sparganium* spp. (Sparganiaceae)
Bushman grass	*Stipagrostis sabulicola*
Capim gordura	*Melinis minutiflora*
Capim-do-campo	*Poa pratensis*
Cheatgrass	*Bromus tectorum*

Chewing's Fescue	*Festuca rubra* ssp. *commutata*
Common bent	*Agrostis capillaris*
Common millet	*Panicum miliaceum*
Common ragwort	*Senecio jacobaea* (Asteraceae)
Common reed	*Phragmites australis*
Cord-grass	*Spartina* spp.
Cotton grasses	*Eriophorum* spp. (Cyperaceae)
Cotton	*Gossypium* spp. (Malvaceae)
Crabgrass	*Digitaria* spp.
Creeping bent	*Agrostis stolonifera*
Crested dogs-tail	*Cynosurus cristatus*
Crocus	*Crocus* spp. (Iridaceae)
Cultivated einkorn	*Triticum monococcum* ssp. *monococcum*
Cultivated emmer	*Triticum turgidum* ssp. *dicoccum*
Daisies	Family Asteraceae
Darnel	*Lolium temulentum*
Deer grasses	*Trichophorum* spp. (Cyperaceae)
Dodder	*Cuscuta* spp. (Convolvulaceae)
Drooping brome	*Bromus tectorum*
Durum wheat	*Triticum turgidum* ssp. *durum*
Dutch grass	*Brachiaria mutica*
Early sand-grass	*Mibora minima*
Einkorn	*Triticum monococcum*
Esparto	*Macrochloa tenacissima* and *Lygeum spartum*
Eyebright	*Euphrasia* spp. (Orobanchaceae)
Fairy club	*Clavaria* spp. (Clavariaceae)
Feather grass	*Stipa* spp.
Fescue	*Festuca* spp.
Finger millet	*Eleusine coracana*
Floating sweet grass	*Glyceria fluitans*
Foxtail millet	*Setaria italica*
Gama grass	*Tripsacum* spp.
Geyser panic grass	*Dichanthelium lanuginosum*
Giant reed	*Arundo donax*
Giant puffball	*Calvatia gigantea* (Lycoperdaceae)
Goat grass	*Aegilops* spp.
Grama de prados	*Poa pratensis*
Grass of Parnassus	*Parnassia palustris* (Parnassiaceae)
Heath grass	*Danthonia* spp.
Highland bent	*Agrostis castellana*
Intermediate wheatgrass	*Thinopyrum intermedium*
Italian ryegrass	*Lolium multiflorum*
Japanese parasol	*Coprinus plicatilis* (Coprinaceae)
Jaraguá grass	*Hyparrhenia rufa*
Job's tears	*Coix lacryma-jobi*
June grass	*Koeleria cristata*

Kentucky bluegrass	*Poa pratensis*
Kikuyu grass	*Pennisetum clandestinum*
Knotgrass	*Polygonum* spp. (Polygonaceae)
Legume	Family Fabaceae
Lily	*Lilium* spp. (Liliaceae)
Little bluestem	*Andropogon scoparius*
Lovegrass	*Eragrostis* spp.
Maize	*Zea mays*
Mallow	Family Malvaceae
Manchurian rice	*Zizania latifolia*
Mango	*Bromus mango*
Marram	*Ammophila arenaria*
Mat grass	*Nardus stricta*
Meadow grass	*Poa* spp.
Millet	*Pennisetum* spp., *Setaria* spp., *Panicum* spp. or *Echinochloa* spp.
Miscanthus	*Miscanthus sinensis*
Molasses grass	*Melinis minutiflora*
Napier grass	*Pennisetum purpureum*
Needle grass	*Aristida* spp.
Noble cane	*Saccharum officinarum*
North American wild rice	*Zizania palustris*
Nutgrass	*Cyperus rotundus* (Cyperaceae)
Oats	*Avena sativa*
Orchid	Family Orchidaceae
Palm	Family Arecaceae
Pampas grass	*Cortaderia selloana*
Papyrus	*Cyperus papyrus* (Cyperaceae)
Pâturin des prés	*Poa pratensis*
Pear bamboo	*Melocanna baccifera*
Pearl millet	*Pennisetum glaucum*
Perennial ryegrass	*Lolium perenne*
Pineapple	*Ananas comosus* (Bromeliaceae)
Pipeweed	Family Eriocaulaceae
Prune	*Prunus domestica* (Rosaceae)
Red fescue	*Festuca rubra*
Reed canary grass	*Phalaris arundinacea*
Reed	*Phragmites* spp.
Reedgrass	*Calamagrostis* spp.
Reedmace	Typha spp. (Typhaceae)
Resurrection grass	*Micraira* spp.
Rhinoceros bush	*Elytropappus rhinocerotis* (Asteraceae)
Rice	*Oryza* spp.
Rough meadow grass	*Poa trivialis*
Rubber tree	*Hevea brasiliensis* (Euphorbiaceae) or *Ficus elastica* (Moraceae)

Rush	Family Juncaceae
Rye	*Secale cereale*
Scleria	*Scleria* spp. (Cyperaceae)
Scorpion-grass	*Myosotis* spp. (Boraginaceae)
Sea oats	*Uniola paniculata*
Sea plantain	*Plantago maritima* (Plantaginaceae)
Sea thrift	*Armeria maritima* (Plumbaginaceae)
Sea-grass	*Zostera* spp. (Zosteraceae)
Sedge	Family Cyperaceae
Sharp rush	*Juncus acutus* (Juncaceae)
Smooth meadow grass	*Poa pratensis*
Soft rush	*Juncus effusus* (Juncaceae)
Sorghum	*Sorghum bicolor*
Spelt	*Triticum aestivum* ssp. *spelta*
Spurges	*Euphorbia* spp. (Euphorbiaceae)
St Augustine grass	*Stenotaphrum secundatum*
Sugar beet	*Beta vulgaris* (Chenopodiaceae)
Sugar maple	*Acer saccharum* (Sapindaceae)
Sugar cane	*Saccharum officinarum*
Sundew	*Drosera* spp. (Droseraceae)
Sweet galingale	*Cyperus longus* (Cyperaceae)
Switchgrass	*Panicum virgatum*
Tef	*Eragrostis tef*
Teosinte	*Zea mays* ssp. *parviglumis*
Three-awn grass	*Aristida* spp.
Timothy grass	*Phleum pratense*
Toadflax	*Linaria* spp. (Plantaginaceae)
Tobacco	*Nicotiana tabacum* (Solanaceae)
Totora	*Schoenoplectus californicus* (Cyperaceae)
Tree lily	Family Velloziaceae
Tufted hairgrass	*Deschampsia cespitosa*
Tulip	*Tulipa* spp. (Liliaceae)
Tussac-grass	*Poa flabellata*
Tussack sedge	*Carex trifida* (Cyperaceae)
Wall barley	*Hordeum murinum*
Waxcap	*Hygrocybe* spp. (Hygrophoraceae)
Wheat	*Triticum* spp.
Wiesen-Rispengras	*Poa pratensis*
Wild einkorn	*Triticum monococcum* ssp. *boeoticum*
Wild emmer	*Triticum turgidum* ssp. *dicoccoides*
Wild rye	*Elymus virginicus*
Witchweed	*Striga* spp. (Orobanchaceae)
Мятлик луговой	*Poa pratensis*

References

📚

1 Dominating the Planet

1 I. Giełwanowska et al., 'Anatomical Features and Ultrastructure of *Deschampsia antarctica* (Poaceae) Leaves from Different Growing Habitats', *Annals of Botany*, 96 (2005), pp. 1109–19; A. Zúñiga-Feest et al., 'Is Survival after Ice Encasement Related with Sugar Distribution in Organs of the Antarctic Plants *Deschampsia antarctica* Desv. (Poaceae) and *Colobanthus quitensis* (Kunth) Bartl. (Caryophyllaceae)?', *Polar Biology*, 32 (2009), pp. 583–91.

2 G. M. Banowetz et al., 'Morphological Adaptations of Hot Springs Panic Grass (*Dichanthelium lanigunosum* var *sericeum* Schmoll) to Thermal Stress', *Journal of Thermal Biology*, 33 (2008), pp. 106–16; R. G. Stout and T. S. Al-Niemi, 'Heat tolerant Flowering Plants of Active Geothermal Areas in Yellowstone National Park', *Annals of Botany*, 90 (2002), pp. 259–67.

3 G. M. Tordoff et al., 'Current Approaches to the Revegetation and Reclamation of Metalliferous Mine Wastes', *Chemosphere*, 41 (2000), pp. 219–28; T. Brej, 'Heavy Metal Tolerance in *Agropyron repens* (L.) P. Bauv. Populations from the Legnica Copper Smelter Area, Lower Silesia', *Acta Societatis Botanicorum Poloniae*, 67 (1998), pp. 325–33.

4 H. L. Piozzi, *Anecdotes of the Late Samuel Johnson, LL.D. During the Last Twenty Years of his Life* (London, 1786), p. 100.

5 N. J. Chaffey, 'Structure and Function of the Membranous Grass Ligule: a Comparative Study', *Botanical Journal of the Linnean Society*, 116 (1994), pp. 53–69.

6 L. G. Clark, 'The Grasses (Poaceae): Robert Brown and Now', *Telopea*, 10 (2004), pp. 505–14.

7 C. J. Whipple et al., 'Conservation of B Class Gene Expression in the Second Whorl of a Basal Grass and Outgroups links the Origin of Lodicules and Petals', *Proceedings of the National Academy of Sciences USA*, 104 (2007), pp. 1081–6.

8 M. W. Chase, 'Monocot Relationships: an Overview', *American Journal of Botany*, 91 (2004), pp. 1645–55.

9   J. I. Davis et al., 'A Phylogeny of the Monocots, as Inferred from *rbc*L and *atp*A Sequence Variation, and a Comparison of Methods for Calculating Jackknife and Bootstrap Values', *Systematic Botany*, 29 (2004), pp. 467–510; M. W. Chase et al., 'Multigene Analysis of Monocot Relationships: A Summary', *Aliso*, 22 (2006), pp. 63–75.

10 A. D. Marchant and B. G. Briggs, 'Ecdeiocoleaceae and Joinvilleaceae, Sisters to Poaceae (Poales): Evidence from *rbc*L and *mat*K Data', *Telopea*, 11 (2007), pp. 437–50.

11 Y. Bouchenak-Khelladi et al., 'Large Multi-gene Phylogenetic Trees of the Grasses (Poaceae): Progress Towards Complete Tribal and Generic Level Sampling', *Molecular Phylogenetics and Evolution*, 47 (2008), pp. 488–505; Z.-Q. Wu and S. Ge, 'The Phylogeny of the BEP Clade in Grasses Revisited: Evidence from the Whole-Genome Sequences of Chloroplasts', *Molecular Phylogenetics and Evolution*, 62 (2012), pp. 573–8.

12 Clark, 'The Grasses (Poaceae)', p. 505.

13 Grass Phylogeny Working Group, 'Phylogeny and Subfamilial Classification of the Grasses (Poaceae)', *Annals of the Missouri Botanical Garden*, 88 (2001), pp. 373–457; Grass Phylogeny Working Group II, 'New Grass Phylogeny Resolves Deep Evolutionary Relationships and Discovers C_4 Origins', *New Phytologist*, 193 (2012), pp. 304–12.

14 W. J. Hooker, *Anomochloa marantoidea*. Maranta-like Anomochloa, *Curtis's Botanical Magazine* (1862), Tab. 5331; L. G. Clark et al., Cleofé E. Calderón (1929–2007), *The Journal of the American Bamboo Society*, 21 (2008), pp. 1–8.

15 A. M. Giulietti et al., *Plantas Raras do Brasil* (Belo Horizonte, 2009), p. 327. E. J. Judziewicz and T. R. Soderstrom, 'Morphological, Anatomical and Taxonomic studies in *Anomochloa* and *Streptochaeta* (Poaceae: Bambusoideae)', *Smithsonian Contributions to Botany*, 68 (1989), pp. 1–51; L. M. Morris and M. R. Duvall, 'The Chloroplast Genome of *Anomochloa marantoidea* (Anomochlooideae; Poaceae) Comprises a Mixture of Grass-like and Unique Features', *American Journal of Botany*, 97 (2010), pp. 620–7.

16 G. Baker, 'Micro-forms of Hay-silica Glass and of Volcanic Glass', *Mineralogical Magazine*, 36 (1968), pp. 1012–23.

17 V. Prasad et al., 'Dinosaur Coprolites and the Early Evolution of Grasses and Grazers', *Science*, 310 (2005), pp. 1177–80; V. Prasad et al., 'Late Cretaceous Origin of the Rice Tribe Provides Evidence for Early Diversification in Poaceae', *Nature Communications*, 2 (2011), doi:10.1038/ncomms1482, accessed 23 December 2011; W. L. Crepet and G. D. Feldman, 'The Earliest Remains of Grasses in the Fossil Record', *American Journal of Botany*, 78 (1991), pp. 1010–14.

18 G. O. Poinar, '*Programinis burmitis* gen. et sp. nov., and *P. laminatus* sp. nov., Early Cretaceous Grass-like Monocots in Burmese Amber', *Australian Systematic Botany*, 17 (2004), pp. 497–504; G. O. Poinar, 'Silica Bodies in the Early Cretaceous *Programinis laminatus* (Angiospermae: Poales)', *Palaeodiversity*, 4 (2011), pp. 1–6.

19 Grass Phylogeny Working Group II, 'New grass phylogeny', pp. 304–12; E.M.V. Nambudiri et al., 'A C_4 Plant from the Pliocene', *Nature*, 276

(1978), pp. 816–17; E. J. Edwards and S. A. Smith, 'Phylogenetic Analyses Reveal the Shady History of C4 Grasses', *Proceedings of the National Academy of Sciences USA*, 107 (2010), pp. 2532–7.

2 Roaming the World

1 D. Johanson and K. Wong, *Lucy's Legacy: The Quest for Human Origins* (New York, 2010); S. Oppenheimer, *Out of Eden: The Peopling of the World* (Johannesburg, 2003); A. Roberts, *The Incredible Human Journey: the Story of How We Colonised the Planet* (London, 2010); C. Stringer and P. Andrews, *The Complete World of Human Evolution* (London, 2011).

2 R. Bond, *A Saga de Aleixo García, o Descobridor do Império Inca* (Florianópolis, 1998); E. Bueno, *Capitães do Brasil: a Saga dos Primeiros Colonizadores* (Rio de Janeiro, 1999).

3 J. A. Boyle, *The Mongol World Empire, 1206–1370* (London, 1977).

4 T. Zerjal et al., 'The Genetic Legacy of the Mongols', *American Journal of Human Genetics*, 72 (2003), pp. 717–21; M. V. Derenko et al., 'Distribution of the Male Lineages of Genghis Khan's Descendants in Northern Eurasian Populations', *Russian Journal of Genetics*, 43 (2007), pp. 334–7.

5 J. E. Weaver and T. J. Fitzpatrick, 'The Prairie', *Ecological Monographs*, 4 (1934), p. 124.

6 J. D. Thomson, *Through Masai Land: a Journey of Exploration Among the Snowclad Volcanic Mountains and Strange Tribes of Eastern Equatorial Africa. Being the Narrative of the Royal Geographical Society's Expedition to Mount Kenia and Lake Victoria Nyanza, 1883–1884* (London, 1887), pp. 91–2. This work inspired Rider Haggard's *King Solomon's Mines* (1885).

7 E. James, *Account of an Expedition from Pittsburgh to the Rocky Mountains, Performed in the Years 1819, 1820* (London, 1823), vol. II, p. 96. This work inspired Fenimore Cooper's *The Prairie: A Tale* (1827).

8 A. Chekov, *The Steppe and Other Stories* (London, 1991), pp. 194, 235.

9 J. E. Keeley and P. W. Rundel, 'Fire and the Miocene Expansion of C_4 Grasslands', *Ecology Letters*, 8 (2005), pp. 683–90.

10 R. M. Laws, 'Elephants as Agents of Habitat and Landscape Change in East Africa', *Oikos*, 21 (1970), pp. 1–15; R. Guldemond and R. van Aarde, 'A Meta-analysis of the Impact of African Elephants on Savanna Vegetation', *The Journal of Wildlife Management*, 72 (2008), pp. 892–9.

11 E. J. Edwards et al., 'The Origins of C_4 Grasslands: Integrating Evolutionary and Ecosystem Science', *Science*, 328 (2010), pp. 587–91.

12 M. Ebner et al., 'Efficient Fog Harvesting by *Stipagrostis sabulicola* (Namib Dune Bushman Grass)', *Journal of Arid Environments*, 75 (2011), pp. 524–31.

13 E. J. Edwards and S. A. Smith, 'Phylogenetic Analyses Reveal the Shady History of C_4 Grasses', *Proceedings of the National Academy of Sciences USA*, 107 (2010): pp. 2532–7.

14 C. Janis, 'An Evolutionary History of Browsing and Grazing Ungulates', in *The Ecology of Browsing and Grazing*, ed. I. J. Gordon and H.H.T. Prins (Berlin, 2008), pp. 21–45.

15 C. M. Janis et al., 'The Origins and Evolution of the North American Grassland Biome: the Story from the Hoofed Mammals', *Palaeogeography, Palaeoclimatology, Palaeoecology*, 177 (2002), pp. 183–98.

16 D. W. Anthony, *The Horse, the Wheel, and Language: How Bronze Age Riders from the Eurasian Steppes Shaped the Modern World* (Princeton, NJ, 2006); S. L. Olsen, 'Early Horse Domestication on the Eurasian Steppe', in M. A. Zeder et al., *Documenting Domestication: New Genetic and Archaeological Paradigms* (Berkeley and Los Angeles, CA, 2006); pp. 245–69.

17 M. B. Coughenour, 'Graminoid Responses to Grazing by Large Herbivores: Adaptations, Exaptations, and Interacting Processes', *Annals of the Missouri Botanical Garden*, 72 (1985), pp. 852–63.

18 A. K. Knapp et al., 'The Keystone Role of Bison in North American Tallgrass Prairie', *BioScience*, 49 (1999), pp. 39–50.

19 N. Schweber, 'As Bison Return to Prairie, Some Rejoice, Others Worry', *New York Times*, 26 April 2012.

20 W. Clark, 'March 30, 1805', in *The Journals of the Lewis and Clark Expedition*, ed. G. Moulton (Lincoln, NE, 2002), http://lewisandclarkjournals.unl.edu, accessed 10 June 2012.

21 J. Goudsblom, 'The Domestication of Fire as a Civilizing Process', *Theory, Culture, Society*, 4 (1987), pp. 457–76.

22 J. E. Keeley and P. W. Rundel, 'Fire and the Miocene Expansion of C_4 Grasslands', *Ecology Letters*, 8 (2005), pp. 683–90.

23 K. F. Higgins, 'Lightning Fires in North Dakota Grasslands and in Pine-Savanna Lands of South Dakota and Montana', *Journal of Range Management*, 37 (1984), pp. 100–103.

24 E. J. Benson et al., 'Belowground Bud Banks and Meristem Limitation in Tallgrass Prairie Plant Populations', *American Journal of Botany*, 91 (2004), pp. 416–21.

25 P. M. Ramsay and E.R.B. Oxley, 'Fire Temperatures and Postfire Plant Community Dynamics in Ecuadorian Grass *Páramo*', *Vegetatio*, 124 (1996), pp. 129–44.

26 Z. Baruch, 'Ecophysiological Aspects of the Invasion of African Grasses and their Impact on Biodiversity and Function of Neotropical Savannas', in *Biodiversity and Savanna Ecosystem Processes: A Global Perspective*, ed. O. T. Solbrig et al. (Berlin, 1996), pp. 79–93.

27 S. Brain, 'The Great Stalin Plan for the Transformation of Nature', *Environmental History*, 15 (2010), pp. 1–31.

28 S. M. Sano et al., *Cerrado. Ecologia e Flora* (Brasília, 2008).

29 J. A. Ratter et al., 'The Brazilian Cerrado Vegetation and Threats to its Biodiversity', *Annals of Botany*, 80 (1997), pp. 223–30.

30 Anonymous, 'The Miracle of the Cerrado', *The Economist*, 26 August 2010. See also letters responding to the article in *The Economist*, 9 September 2010.

31 D. Pimentel et al., 'Environmental and Economic Costs of Soil Erosion and Conservation Benefits', *Science*, 267 (1995), pp. 1117–23.

3 Disguising Grasses

1 M. W. Chase et al., 'Multigene Analysis of Monocot Relationships: A Summary', *Aliso*, 22 (2006), pp. 63–75.

2 G. White, *The Natural History and Antiquities of Selborne, with Observations on Various Parts of Nature, and the Naturalist's Calendar* (London, 1853), letter 26, dated 1 November 1775.

3 A. Burton, *Rush-bearing: An Account of the Old Custom of Strewing Rushes: Carrying Rushes to Church; the Rush-cart; Garlands in Churches; Morris-dancers; the Wakes; the Rush* (Manchester, 1891).

4 H. J. Scoggan, *The Flora of Canada. Part 1. General Survey* (Ottawa, 1978); A. E. Porsild and W. J. Cody, *Vascular Plants of Continental Northwest Territories, Canada* (Ottawa, 1980).

5 G. C. Druce, '*Carex microglochin* Wahlenberg', *Botanical Exchange Club Report*, 1923 (1924), pp. 1–3.

6 G. A. Wheeler and E. R. Guaglianone, 'Notes on South American *Carex* (Cyperaceae): *C. camptoglochin* and *C. microglochin*', *Darwiniana*, 41 (2003), pp. 193–206.

7 R. Parkinson and S. Quirke, *Papyrus* (London, 1995).

8 C. Bronk Ramsey et al., 'Radiocarbon-Based Chronology for Dynastic Egypt', *Science*, 328 (2010), pp. 1554–7.

9 T. Heyerdahl, *The Ra Expeditions* (London, 1993).

10 E. S. Forster, 'Trees and Plants in Herodotus', *Classical Review*, 56 (1942), pp. 57–63.

11 In an engaging parable, D. Isley ('The Disappearance', *Taxon*, 21 (1972), pp. 3–12) makes a case for the importance of taxonomy. Although the text is dated, the ideas are as relevant now as they were 40 years ago.

12 J. R. Forster, *Voyage Around the World. Performed by Order of his Most Christian Majesty, in the Years 1766, 1767, 1768, and 1769, by Lewis de Bougainville* (London, 1772), p. 51.

13 Hooker, 'Notes on the Botany', p. 294.

14 P. Thoday, *Two Blades of Grass: The Story of Cultivation* (Corsham, Wiltshire, 2007).

4 Civilizing Humans

1 M. W. van Slageren, *Wild Wheats: A Monograph of Aegilops L. and Amblyopyrum (Jaub. & Spach) Eig (Poaceae)* (Wageningen, 1994).

2 A. A. Levy and M. Feldman, 'Genetic and Epigenetic Reprogramming of the Wheat Genome Upon Allopolyploidisation', *Biological Journal of the Linnean Society*, 82 (2005), pp. 607–15.

3 M. Heun et al., 'A Critical Review of the Protracted Domestication Model for Near-Eastern Founder Crops: Linear Regression, Long-distance Gene Flow, Archaeological, and Archaeobotanical Evidence', *Journal of Experimental Botany*, 63 (2012), 695–709.

4 D. L. Martin and A. H. Goodman, 'Health Conditions Before Columbus: Paleopathology of Native North Americans', *Western Journal of Medicine*, 176 (2002), pp. 65–8; E. A. Pechenkina et al., 'Diet and Health Changes at the End of the Chinese Neolithic: the Yangshao/Longshan Transition in Shaanxi Province', *American Journal of Physical Anthropology*, 117 (2002), pp. 15–36.

5 J. D. Rudney, 'Dental Indicators or Growth Disturbance in a Series of Ancient Lower Nubian Populations: Changes Over Time', *American Journal of Physical Anthropology*, 60 (1982), pp. 463–70.

6 C. L. Brace et al., 'What Big Teeth You Had Grandma! Human Tooth Size Past and Present', in *Advances in Dental Anthropology*, ed. M. A. Kelley and C. S. Larsen (New York, 1991), pp. 33–56.

7 A. Mummert et al., 'Stature and Robusticity During the Agricultural Transition: Evidence from the Bioarchaeological Record', *Economics and Human Biology*, 9 (2011), pp. 284–301.

8 N. G. Jablonski and G. Chaplin, 'Human Skin Pigmentation as an Adaptation to UV Radiation', *Proceedings of the National Academy of Sciences USA*, 107 (2010), pp. 8962–8.

9 C. Holden and R. Mace, 'Phylogenetic Analysis of the Evolution of Lactose Digestion in Adults', *Human Biology*, 69 (1997), pp. 605–28.

10 A. Keller et al., 'New Insights into the Tyrolean Iceman's Origin and Phenotype as Inferred by Whole-Genome Sequencing', *Nature Communications*, 3 (2012), DOI: doi:10.1038/ncomms1701.

11 C.J.E. Ingram et al., 'A Novel Polymorphism Associated with Lactose Tolerance in Africa: Multiple Causes for Lactase Persistence?', *Human Genetics*, 120 (2007), pp. 779–88.

12 W. Ridgeway, *The Origin of Metallic Currency and Weight Standards* (Cambridge, 1892), pp. 180–81.

13 Estimated from global production data reported by FAOSTAT (2012), www.faostat.fao.org, accessed 1 April 2012.

5 Confusing Botanists

1 P. H. Smith and P. Findlen, *Merchants and Marvels: Commerce, Science, and Art in Early Modern Europe* (London, 2002); L. Daston and K. Park, *Wonders and the Order of Nature, 1150–1750* (New York, 2001).

2 W. H. Prescott, *History of the Conquest of Mexico* (London, 1854), vol. II, p. 129. The emphasis is Prescott's.

3 J. Gerard, *The Herball or Generall Historie of Plantes* (London, 1597), p. 77.

4 H. Lyte, *A Nievve Herball or Historie of Plantes* (London, 1578), p. 463.

5 The word 'maize' is used here in preference to 'corn' for two reasons: (i) contemporarily and historically, people use 'corn' to refer to their own most important cereal; and (ii) 'corn' in North America has come to mean maize with large, yellow, sweet kernels.

6 Lyte, *A Nievve Herball*, p. 464.

7 Ibid.

8 Gerard, *The Herball*, pp. 75–6.

9 C. O. Sauer, *Maize in Europe. Akten des 34* (Vienna, 1960), pp. 778–86.

10 A. de Candolle, 'Histoire. Histoire Naturelle, Agricole et Economique du Maïs, par M. Matthieu Bonafous', *Annales de l'agriculture française*, 19 (1837), pp. 5–27. M. Bonafous, *Histoire Naturelle, Agricole et Economique du Maïs*, 2nd edn (Paris, 1836). P. A. Browne, *An Essay on Indian Corn* (Philadelphia, PA, 1837).

11 P. Weatherwax, *The Story of the Maize Plant* (Chicago, IL, 1923).

12 Sauer, *Maize in Europe*, pp. 778–86.

13 J. Ruellius, *De Natura Stirpium Libri Tres* (Paris, 1536), p. 428, line 34. Assuming a human generation time of 25 years, this would imply a pre-Columbian Old World occurrence of maize.

14 K. Kunz and G. Sigurdsson, *The Vinland Sagas* (London, 2008), pp. 35, 44.

15 E. L. Sturtevant, 'Indian Corn and the Indian', *American Naturalist*, 19 (1885), pp. 225–34. Kunz and Sigurdsson, *The Vinland Sagas*, p. 56, fn. 11, suggest that the grasses were either wild rice or wild rye.

16 K. Taube, *Aztec and Maya Myths* (Austin, TX, 1993).

17 P. C. Mangelsdorf and R. G. Reeves, 'The Origin of Indian Corn and its Relatives', *Texas Agricultural Experimental Station Bulletin* (1939), p. 574; P. C. Mangelsdorf, 'The Origin and Evolution of Maize', *Advances in Genetics*, 1 (1947), pp. 161–207; P. C. Mangelsdorf, *Corn: its Origin, Evolution and Improvement* (Cambridge, MA, 1974).

18 B. F. Benz and H. Iltis, 'Studies in Archaeological Maize I: The 'Wild' Maize from the San Marcos Cave Reexamined', *American Antiquity*, 55 (1990), pp. 500–511.

19 J. Bennetzen et al., 'Genetic Evidence and the Origin of Maize', *Latin American Antiquity*, 12 (2001), pp. 84–6.

20 G. W. Beadle, 'Teosinte and the Origin of Maize', *Journal of Heredity*, 30 (1939), pp. 245–7.

21 V. Jaenicke-Després et al., 'Early Allelic Selection in Maize as Revealed by Ancient DNA', *Science*, 302 (2003), pp. 1206–8; A. Eyre-Walker et al., 'Investigation of the Bottleneck Leading to the Domestication of Maize', *Proceedings of the National Academy of Sciences USA*, 95 (1998), pp. 4441–6.

22 J. Doebley, 'The Genetics of Maize Evolution', *Annual Review of Genetics*, 38 (2004), pp. 37–59.

23 B. F. Benz, 'Archaeological Evidence of Teosinte Domestication of Guilá Naquitz, Oaxaca', *Proceedings of the National Academy of Sciences USA*, 98 (2001), pp. 2104–6; D. R. Piperno and K. V. Flannery, 'The Earliest Archaeological Maize (*Zea mays* L.) from Highland Mexico: New Accelerator Mass Spectrometry Dates and Their Implication', *Proceedings of the National Academy of Sciences USA*, 98 (2001), pp. 2101–3.

24 Y. Matsuoka et al., 'A Single Domestication for Maize Shown by Multilocus Microsatellite Genotyping', *Proceedings of the National Academy of Sciences USA*, 99 (2002), pp. 6080–4.

25 B. B. Huckell, 'The Archaic Prehistory of the North American Southwest', *Journal of World Prehistory*, 10 (1996), pp. 305–73; B. D. Smith, 'Origins of

Agriculture in Eastern North America', *Science*, 246 (1989), pp. 1556–71; C. C. Mann, *The Americas before Columbus* (London, 2006).

6 Feeding Humans

1 U. Deichmann, *Biologists Under Hitler* (Cambridge, MA, 1996); T. Wieland, 'Autarky and *Lebensraum*: The Political Agenda of Academic Plant Breeding in Nazi Germany', *Journal of History of Science and Technology*, 3 (2009).

2 K. Borojevic and K. Borojevic, 'The Transfer and History of "Reduced Height Genes" (rht) in Wheat from Japan to Europe', *Journal of Heredity*, 96 (2005), pp. 455–9.

3 M. Kremer, 'Population Growth and Technological Change: One Million B.C. to 1990', *Quarterly Journal of Economics*, 108 (1993), pp. 681–716; J. Coleman, 'World's "Seven Billionth Baby" is Born', *The Guardian*, 31 October 2011.

4 T. Jacobsen and R. M. Adams, 'Salt and Silt in Ancient Mesopotamian Agriculture', *Science*, 128 (1958), pp. 1251–8; C. N. Runnels, 'Environmental Degradation in Ancient Greece', *Scientific American*, 272 (1995), pp. 72–5.

5 S. C. Walpole et al., 'The Weight of Nations: an Estimation of Adult Human Biomass', BMC *Public Health*, 12 (2012), doi:10.1186/1471-2458-12-439.

6 D. Dawe, 'Agricultural Research, Poverty Alleviation and Key Trends in Asia's Rice Economy', in *Charting New Pathways to C4 Rice*, ed. J. E. Sheehy et al. (Singapore, 2007), pp. 37–53.

7 M. Sweeney and S. McCouch, 'The Complex History of the Domestication of Rice', *Annals of Botany*, 100 (2007), pp. 951–7; D. Q. Fuller et al., 'Consilience of Genetics and Archaeobotany in the Entangled History of Rice', *Archaeological and Anthropological Sciences*, 2 (2010), pp. 115–31.

8 J. Molina et al., 'Molecular Evidence for a Single Evolutionary Origin of Domesticated Rice', *Proceedings of the National Academy of Sciences USA*, 108 (2011), pp. 8351–6.

9 International Rice Genome Sequencing Project, 'The Map-based Sequence of the Rice Genome', *Nature*, 436 (2005), pp. 793–800.

10 C. Li et al., 'Rice Domestication by Reducing Shattering', *Science*, 311 (2006), pp. 1936–9.

11 J. A. Carney, *Black Rice: The African Origins of Rice Cultivation in the Americas* (Cambridge, MA, 2001); J. A. Carney and R. N. Rosomoff, *In the Shadow of Slavery: Africa's Botanical Legacy in the Atlantic World* (Berkeley, CA, 2009).

12 Z. M. Li et al., 'Genetic Diversity and Domestication History of African Rice (*Oryza glaberrima*) as Inferred from Multiple Gene Sequences', *Theoretical and Applied Genetics*, 123 (2011), pp. 21–31; R. Portères, *Primary Cradles of Agriculture in the African Continent* (Cambridge, 1970); P. Richards, *Redefining Nature: Ecology, Culture and Domestication* (Oxford, 1996).

13 O. F. Linares, 'African Rice (*Oryza glaberrima*): History and Future Potential', *Proceedings of the National Academy of Sciences USA*, 99 (2002), pp. 16360–5; Li et al., 'Genetic Diversity and Domestication History of African Rice', pp. 21–31.

14　D. E. Moerman, *North American Ethnobotany* (Portland, OR, 1998), p. 614.

15　H. B. Guo et al., 'Zizania latifolia Turcz. Cultivated in China', *Genetic Resources and Crop Evolution*, 54 (2007), pp. 1211–7.

16　A. Reid, *Leningrad: Tragedy of a City Under Siege, 1941–44* (London, 2011).

17　T. Hargrove and W. R. Coffman, 'Breeding History', *Rice Today*, 5 (2005), pp. 34–8.

18　C. W. Dugger, 'In Africa, Holy Grail for Hunger is a New Rice', *International Herald Tribune*, 9 October 2007.

19　P. Beyer, 'Golden Rice and "Golden" Crops for Human Nutrition', *New Biotechnology*, 27 (2010), pp. 478–81.

20　D. F. Robinson, *Confronting Biopiracy: Challenges, Cases and International Debates* (London, 2010), pp. 47–9, 66–7.

7 Sweetening Life

1　J. N. Warner, 'Sugar Cane: an Indigenous Papuan Cultigen', *Ethnology*, 1 (1962), pp. 405–11.

2　L. Gopal, 'Sugar-making in Ancient India', *Journal of the Economic and Social History of the Orient*, 7 (1964), pp. 57–72.

3　T. Salmon, *Modern History: or, the Present State of all Nations* (London, 1746), p. 397.

4　MS Sherard 219, f.226r (Sherard Library, Bodleian Library).

5　N. Deerr, *The History of Sugar* (London, 1949–50).

6　G. R. Horst et al., 'The Mongoose in the West Indies: The Biogeography and Population Biology of an Introduced Species', in *Biogeography of the West Indies: Patterns and Perspectives*, ed. C. A. Woods and F. E. Sergile (Boca Raton, FL, 2001), pp. 409–24.

7　J. Gerard, *The Herball or General Historie of Plantes* (London, 1597), p. 35.

8　B. Kiernan, *Blood and Soil: A World History of Genocide and Extermination from Sparta to Darfur* (New Haven, CT, 2007).

9　Moseley, *A Treatise on Sugar*, p. 157.

10　Gerard, *The Herball*, p. 35.

11　Voltaire, *Candide, ou L'optimisme, Traduit de l'Allemand de M. le Docteur Ralph* (Paris, 1759), p. 127.

12　Moseley, *A Treatise on Sugar*, p. 38.

13　J. B. Debret, *Voyage Pictoresque et Historique au Brésil* (Paris, 1835), vol. II, pls 25 and 24; J. D. Bandeira and P. Corrêa do Lago, *Debret e o Brasil. Obra Completa 1816–1831* (São Paulo, 2008).

14　M. C. Eakin, *British Enterprise in Brazil: The St. John d'el Rey Mining Company and the Morro Velho Gold Mine, 1830–1960* (London, 1989). M. D. Childs, 'A Case of "Great Unstableness": A British Slaveholder and Brazilian Abolition', *The Historian*, 60 (1998), pp. 717–40.

15　C. Darwin, *The Origin of Species and the Voyage of the Beagle* (London, 2003), p. 509.

16　Moseley, *A Treatise on Sugar*, p. 140.

17　Ibid., p. 152.

18 B. A. Weinberg and B. K. Bealer, *The World of Caffeine: The Science and Culture of the World's Most Popular Drug* (London, 2002).

19 G. Freyre, *Casa Grande e Senzala* (São Paulo, 2006).

8 Protecting the Crop

1 H. R. Fairclough, *Virgil: Georgics* (Cambridge, MA, 1999), Book I, 150–51. In this translation 'robigo' was translated as 'mildew', although it is perhaps better translated as 'rust'.

2 R. G. Wasson et al., *The Road to Eleusis: Unveiling the Secrets of the Mysteries* (New York, 1978).

3 W. W. Fowler, *The Roman Festivals of the Period of the Republic* (London, 1908).

4 J. G. Frazer, *Ovid: Fasti* (Cambridge, MA, 1931), Book 4, lines 901–42.

5 L. A. Tatum, 'The Southern Corn Leaf Blight Epidemic', *Science*, 171 (1971), pp. 1113–16; A. J. Ullstrup, 'The Impacts of the Southern Corn Leaf Blight Epidemics of 1970–1971', *Annual Review of Phytopathology*, 10 (1972), pp. 37–50.

6 M. R. Lee, 'The History of Ergot of Rye (*Claviceps purpurea*) I: From Antiquity to 1900', *Journal of the Royal College of Physicians Edinburgh*, 39 (2009), pp. 179–84.

7 G. Barger, *Ergot and Ergotism* (London, 1931), p. 44. This figure is remarkably high, and Barger suggests that there may have been confusion with bubonic plague.

8 D. Dodart, 'Lettre de M. Dodart de L'Academie Royalle des Sciences, a l'Auteur du Journal Contenant des Choses Fort Remarquables Touchant Quelques-Grains', *Le Journal des Sçavans*, 10 (1676), pp. 69–72.

9 L. R. Tulasne, 'Mémoire Sur l'Ergot des Glumacées', *Annales de Science Naturelle* Botanique, 3 (1853), pp. 5–56.

10 V. Křen and L. Cvak, *Ergot: The Genus* Claviceps (Amsterdam, 2005).

11 K. Duncan, 'Was Ergotism Responsible for the Scottish Witch-hunts?', *Area*, 25 (1993), pp. 30–36.

12 L. R. Caporael, 'Ergotism: the Satan Loosed in Salem?', *Science*, 192 (1976), pp. 21–6. For the counter arguments see N. P. Spanos and J. Gottlieb, 'Ergotism and the Salem Village Witch Trials', *Science*, 194 (1976), pp. 1390–94 and A. Woolf, 'Witchcraft or Mycotoxin? The Salem Witch Trials', *Journal of Toxicology and Clinical Toxicology*, 38 (2000), pp. 457–60.

13 K. Akiyama and H. Hayashi, 'Strigolactones: Chemical Signals for Fungal Symbionts and Parasitic Weeds in Plant Roots', *Annals of Botany*, 97 (2006), pp. 925–31.

14 FAO (2012) FAOSTAT, faostat.fao.org, accessed 1 April 2012.

15 E. H. Fulling, 'Plant Life and the Law of Man. IV. Barberry, Currant and Gooseberry, and Cedar Control', *Botanical Review*, 9 (1943), pp. 483–592.

16 M. Grieve, *A Modern Herbal. The Medicinal, Culinary, Cosmetic and Economic Properties, Cultivation and Folklore of Herbs, Grasses, Fungi, Shrubs and Trees with all their Modern Scientific Names* (London, 1931), pp. 82–4; D. E. Allen and G. Hatfield, *Medicinal Plants in Folk Traditions: An Ethnobotany of Britain and Ireland*

(Portland, OR, 2004), p. 76.

17 The statement about the Edict of Rouen is widely repeated and appears to be based on a single report in H. von Klebahm, *Die Wirtswechselnden Rostpilze: Versuch Einer Gesamtdarstellung Ihrer Biologischen Verhältnisse* (Berlin, 1904), p. 205, which in turn was based on a secondary French source. There is no direct evidence that the law was ever introduced.

18 Fulling, 'Plant Life and the Law of Man', pp. 483–92; P. W. Bidwell and J. I. Falconer, *History of Agriculture in the Northern United States, 1620–1880* (Washington, DC, 1925).

19 R. Hogg, *The Vegetable Kingdom and its Products* (London, 1858), p. 35.

20 A. De Bary, 'Neue Untersuchungen über die Uredineen, Inbesondere die Entwicklung der *Puccinia graminis* und den Zusammenhang Derselben mit *Aecidium Berberidis*', *Monatsbericht der Königlich-Preussischen Akademie der Wissenschaften zu Berlin*, 1865 (1865), pp. 15–49.

21 R. P. Singh et al., 'The Emergence of Ug99 Races of the Stem Rust Fungus is a Threat to World Wheat Production', *Annual Review of Phytopathology*, 49 (2011), pp. 465–81.

22 H. Leung et al., 'Using Genetic Diversity to Achieve Sustainable Rice Disease Management', *Plant Disease*, 87 (2003), pp. 1156–69.

23 M. Tester, and P. Langridge, 'Breeding Technologies to Increase Crop Production in a Changing World', *Science*, 327 (2010), pp. 818–22.

24 D. Burke, 'GM Food and Crops: What Went Wrong in the UK?', *EMBO Reporter*, 5 (2004), pp. 432–6.

25 Singh, 'The Emergence of Ug99 Races', pp. 465–81.

26 W. Remy et al., '4 Hundred Million Year Old Vesicular-arbuscular Mycorrhizae', *Proceeding of the National Academy of Sciences USA*, 91 (1994), pp. 11841–3.

27 B. Wang and Y. L. Qiu, 'Phylogenetic Distribution and Evolution of Mycorrhizas in Land Plants', *Mycorrhiza*, 16 (2006), pp. 299–363.

28 P. Šmilauer, 'Communities of Arbuscular Mycorrhizal Fungi in Grassland: Seasonal Variability and Effects of Environment and Host Plants', *Folia Geobotanica*, 36 (2001), pp. 243–63; M. A. Lugo and M. N. Cabello, 'Native Arbuscular Mycorrhizal Fungi (AMF) from Mountain Grassland (Córdoba, Argentina) I. Seasonal Variation of Fungal Spore Diversity', *Mycologia*, 94 (2002), pp. 579–86; M. A. Lugo et al., 'Arbuscular Mycorrhizal Fungi in a Mountain Grassland II: Seasonal Variation of Colonization Studied, Along with its Relation to Grazing and Metabolic Host Type', *Mycologia*, 95 (2003), pp. 407–15; J. Wehner et al., 'Indigenous Arbuscular Mycorrhizal Fungal Assemblages Protect Grassland Host Plants from Pathogens', *PLOS ONE*, 6 (2011), e27381.

29 I. M. Cardoso and T. W. Kuyper, 'Mycorrhizas and Tropical Soil Fertility', *Agriculture, Ecosystems & Environment*, 116 (2006), pp. 72–84.

30 L. M. Márquez et al., 'A Virus in a Fungus in a Plant: Three-way Symbiosis Required for Thermal Tolerance', *Science*, 315 (2007), pp. 513–15.

31 L. H. Rosa et al., 'Endophytic Fungi Associated with the Antarctic Grass *Deschampsia antarctica* Desv. (Poaceae)', *Polar Biology*, 32 (2009), pp. 161–7.

32 D. Cavalieri, 'Evidence for *S. cerevisiae* Fermentation in Ancient Wine', *Journal of Molecular Evolution*, 57 (2003), pp. S226–32.

33 R. J. Braidwood et al., 'Symposium: Did Man Once Live by Beer Alone?', *American Anthropologist*, 55 (1953), pp. 515–26.

34 K. L. Manchester, 'Louis Pasteur (1822–1895) – Chance and the Prepared Mind', *Trends in Biotechnology*, 13 (1995), pp. 511–5.

35 I. Gately, *Drink: A Cultural History of Alcohol* (New York, 2009); G. Oliver and T. Colicchio, *The Oxford Companion to Beer* (Oxford, 2011); T. Bruce-Gardyne and G. Satterley, *The Scotch Whisky Book* (Edinburgh, 2002).

36 M. Valverde, *Diseases of the Will: Alcohol and the Dilemmas of Freedom* (Cambridge, 1998).

37 Gately, *Drink*.

38 P. Dillon, *The Much-lamented Death of Madam Geneva* (London, 2002).

39 B. A. Weinberg and B. K. Bealer, *The World of Caffeine: The Science and Culture of the World's Most Popular Drug* (London, 2002).

40 G. Gardner, *Travels in the Interior of Brazil, Principally Through the Northern Provinces and the Gold and Diamond Districts, During the Years 1836–1841* (London, 1846).

41 R. F. Burton, *Exploration of the Highlands of Brazil; a Full Account of the Gold and Diamond Mines, also, Canoeing Down 1500 Miles of the Great River São Francisco, from Sabará to the Sea* (London, 1869), vol. I, p. 189.

42 R. Conniff, *The Species Seekers: Heroes, Fools, and the Mad Pursuit of Life on Earth* (London, 2011).

9 Foraging the Fields

1 R. Turvey, 'Horse Traction in Victorian London', *Journal of Transport History*, 26 (2005), pp. 38–59.

2 FAOSTAT (2012), faostat.fao.org, accessed 13 November 2012; A. Pearson et al., eds, *Working Animals in Agriculture and Transport. A Collection or Current Research and Development Observations* (Wageningen, 2003).

3 S. Johnson, *A Dictionary of the English Language* (London, 1755).

4 E. J. T. Collins, 'Dietary Change and Cereal Consumption in Britain in the Nineteenth Century', *Agricultural History Review*, 23 (1975), pp. 97–115.

5 T. D. Hall, 'South African Pastures: Retrospective and Prospective', *South African Journal of Science*, 31 (1932), pp. 59–97. A. J. H. Goodwin, 'Jan van Riebeck and the Hottentots 1652–1662', *South African Archaeological Bulletin*, 7 (1952), pp. 7–53; S. Pooley, 'Jan van Riebeeck as Pioneering Explorer and Conservator of Natural Resources at the Cape of Good Hope (1652–62)', *Environment and History*, 15 (2009), pp. 3–33; J. van Riebeeck and R. Kirby, *The Secret Letters of Jan van Riebeeck* (Harmondsworth, 1992).

6 Goodwin, 'Jan van Riebeck', p. 10.

7 Ibid., p. 18.

8 Pooley, 'Jan van Riebeeck', pp. 3–33.

9 T. D. Hall, 'South African Pastures: Retrospective and Prospective', *South African Journal of Science*, 31 (1932), pp. 59–97.

10 R. Ross, *A Concise History of South Africa*, 2nd edn (Cambridge, 2008).

11 S. Hartlib, *Samuel Hartlib his Legacie: or an Enlargement of the Discourse of Husbandry used in Brabant and Flaunders; Wherein are Bequeathed to the Common-Wealth of England More Outlandish and Domestick Experiments and Secrets in Reference to Universal Husbandry* (London, 1651), p. 47.

12 M. Lamer, *The World Fertilizer Economy* (Stanford, CA, 1957).

13 R. G. Jefferson, 'The Conservation Management of Upland Hay Meadows in Britain: A Review', *Grass and Forage Science*, 60 (2005), pp. 322–31.

14 C. J. Stevens et al., 'Impact of Nitrogen Deposition on the Species Richness of Grasslands', *Science*, 303 (2004), 1876–9; C. M. Clark and D. Tilman, Loss of Plant Species after Chronic Low-level Nitrogen Deposition to Prairie Grasslands', *Nature*, 451 (2008), pp. 712–15.

15 Z. Hrevušová et al., 'Long-term Dynamics of Biomass Production, Soil Chemical Properties and Plant Species Composition of Alluvial Grassland After the Cessation of Fertilizer Application in the Czech Republic', *Agriculture, Ecosystems and Environment*, 130 (2009), pp. 123–30; D. Honsová et al., 'Species Composition of an Alluvial Meadow After 40 Years of Applying Nitrogen, Phospohorus [*sic*] and Potassium Fertilizer', *Preslia*, 79 (2007), pp. 245–58.

16 J. Silvertown et al., 'The Park Grass Experiment 1856–2006: Its Contribution to Ecology', *Journal of Ecology*, 94 (2006), pp. 801–14.

10 Making a Future

1 T.-H. Tsien, 'Raw Materials for Old Papermaking in China', *Journal of the American Oriental Society*, 93 (1973), pp. 510–19.

2 J. D. Hansom, 'Sandy Beaches and Dunes – GCR Site Reports. Tentsmuir (GCR ID: 1070)', in *Coastal Geomorphology of Great Britain*, ed. J. D. Hansom (London, 2003), p. 2731.

3 M. A. Maun, *The Biology of Coastal Sand Dunes* (Oxford, 2009).

4 L. D. Carter, 'A Pleistocene Sand Sea on the Alaskan Arctic Coastal Plain', *Science*, 211 (1981), pp. 381–3.

5 J. L. Knapp, *Gramina Britannica*. G. Sinclair, *Hortus Gramineus Woburnensis* (London, 1824).

6 V.H.D. Zuazo and C.R.R. Pleguezuelo, 'Soil-erosion and Runoff Prevention by Plant Covers: A Review', in *Sustainable Agriculture*, ed. E. Lichtfouse et al. (Dordrecht, 2009), pp. 785–811; D. Pimentel et al., 'Environmental and Economic Costs of Soil Erosion and Conservation Benefits', *Science*, 267 (1995), pp. 1117–23.

7 L. Xing-Hua et al., 'Copper Tolerance of the Biomass Crops Elephant Grass (*Pennisetum purpureum* Schumach), Vetiver grass (*Vetiveria zizanioides*) and the Upland Reed (*Phragmites australis*) in Soil Culture', *Biotechnology Advances*, 27 (2009), pp. 633–40; J. M. Ayotamunoa et al., 'Composting and Phytoremediation Treatment of Petroleum Sludge', *Soil and Sediment Contamination: An International Journal*, 19 (2010), pp. 686–95.

8 J. Vymazal, 'Constructed Wetlands for Wastewater Treatment', *Water*, 2 (2010), pp. 530–49.

9 International Energy Agency, *Technology Roadmap. Biofuels for Transport* (Paris, 2011).

10 The Brazil Institute, *The Global Dynamics of Biofuels. Potential Supply and Demand for Ethanol and Biodiesel in the Coming Decade* (Washington, DC, 2007).

11 R. Saidur et al., 'A Review on Biomass as a Fuel for Boilers', *Renewable and Sustainable Energy Reviews*, 15 (2011), pp. 2262–89.

12 S. N. Naik et al., 'Production of First and Second Generation Biofuels: A Comprehensive Review', *Renewable and Sustainable Energy Reviews*, 14 (2010), pp. 578–97.

13 Nuffield Council on Bioethics, *Biofuels: Ethical Issues* (London, 2011).

14 G. Gardner, *Travels in the Interior of Brazil, Principally Through the Northern Provinces and the Gold and Diamond Districts, During the Years 1836–1841* (London, 1846).

15 P. Russell, 'An Account of the Tabasheer', *Philosophical Transactions of the Royal Society of London*, 80 (1790), pp. 273–83; D. Brewster, 'On the Natural History and Properties of Tabasheer, the Siliceous Concretion in the Bamboo', *Edinburgh Journal of the Sciences*, 8 (1828), pp. 285–94.

16 M. N. Somleva, 'Production of Polyhydroxybutyrate in Switchgrass, a Value-added Co-product in an Important Lignocellulosic Biomass Crop', *Plant Biotechnology Journal*, 6 (2008), pp. 663–78.

11 Playing the Field

1 C. E. Hubbard, *Grasses: A Guide to Their Structure, Identification, Uses and Distribution in the British Isles*, 3rd edn (London, 1984), p. 432.

2 J. Brown, *Lancelot 'Capability' Brown: The Omnipotent Magician, 1716–1783* (London, 2011).

3 F. Ginn, 'Dig for Victory! New Histories of Wartime Gardening in Britain', *Journal of Historical Geography*, 38 (2012), pp. 294–305.

4 J. Black, 'Vegetable Garden will be Installed on White House Grounds', *Washington Post*, 20 March 2009.

5 J. Vasagar, 'School Playing Field Sell-offs Continue to Rise', *The Guardian*, 7 August 2012.

6 Milesi et al., 'Mapping and Modeling the Biogeochemical Cycling', pp. 426–38.

7 C. Darwin, *The Formation of Vegetable Mould, Through the Action of Worms, With Observations on Their Habits* (London, 1881), p. 313.

12 Tramping the World

1 H. Rackham, *Pliny: Natural History. Books 17–19* (London, 1997), Book 18, 44.

2 M. Treub, 'Notice Sur la Nouvelle Flore de Krakatau', *Annales du Jardin botanique de Buitenzorg*, 7 (1888), pp. 213–23. Treub's hypothesis that Krakatau was sterilized after the explosion was strongly challenged by C. A. Backer, *The Problem of Krakatoa as Seen by a Botanist* (privately published, 1929).

3 G. Gardner, *Travels in the Interior of Brazil, Principally Through the Northern Provinces and the Gold and Diamond Districts, During the Years 1836–1841* (London, 1846), p. 477.

4 P. G. Lemaux, 'Genetically Engineered Plants and Foods: A Scientist's Analysis of the Issues (Part II)', *Annual Review of Plant Biology*, 60 (2009), pp. 511–59.

5 J. R. Reichman and L. S. Watrud, 'Identification of Escaped Transgenic Creeping Bentgrass in Oregon', *isb News Reporter* (April 2007), pp. 1–4; J. R. Reichman et al., 'Establishment of Transgenic Herbicide-resistant Creeping Bentgrass (*Agrostis stolonifera* L.) in Non-agronomic Habitats', *Molecular Ecology*, 15 (2006), pp. 4243–55.

6 W. S. Blatchley, *The Indiana Weed Book* (Indianapolis, IN, 1912); R. P. Wodehouse, 'Weed', *Encyclopaedia Britanica*, 23 (1960), pp. 477–9.

7 Blatchley, *The Indiana Weed Book*. T. Pritchard, 'Race Formation in Weedy Species with Special Reference to *Euphorbia cyparissus* L. and *Hypericum perforatum* L.', in *The Biology of Weeds*, ed. J. L. Harper (Oxford, 1960), pp. 61–6.

8 W. M. Lush, 'Biology of *Poa annua* in a Temperature Zone Golf Putting Green (*Agrostis stolonifera/Poa annua*). I. The Above-ground Population', *Journal of Applied Ecology*, 25 (1988), pp. 977–88.

9 M. Williamson, *Biological Invasions* (London, 1996).

10 R. N. Mack and D. A. Pyke, 'The Demography of *Bromus tectorum*: Variation in Time and Space', *Journal of Ecology*, 71 (1983), pp. 69–93.

11 A. Leopold, 'Cheat Takes Over', *The Land*, 1 (1941), pp. 310–13.

12 Mack and Pyke, 'The Demography of *Bromus tectorum*'.

13 I. M. Hayward and G. C. Druce, *The Adventive Flora of Tweedside* (Arbroath, 1919), p. 267.

14 I. Silberbauer-Gottsberger, 'Fruit Dispersal and Trypanocarpy in Brazilian Cerrado Grasses', *Plant Systematics and Evolution*, 147 (1984), pp. 1–27.

15 T. B. Ryves et al., *Alien Grasses of the British Isles* (London, 1996).

16 W. J. Hooker, 'Notes on the Botany of HM Discovery Ships, Erebus and Terror in the Antarctic Voyage; With Some Account of the Tussac Grass of the Falklands', *London Journal of Botany*, 2 (1843), p. 280.

17 T. Cope and A. Gray, *Grasses of the British Isles* (London, 2009).

18 S.C.H. Barrett, 'Genetics of Weeds Invasions', *Applied Population Biology*, ed. S. K. Jain and L. W. Botsford (Amsterdam, 1992), pp. 91–199; S. McIntyre and S.C.H. Barrett, 'A Comparison of Weed Communities of Rice in Australia and California', *Proceedings of the Ecological Society, Australia*, 14 (1986), pp. 237–50.

19 R. G. Wasson et al., *The Road to Eleusis: Unveiling the Secret of the Mysteries* (Berkeley, CA, 2008).

20 J. Gerard, *The Herball or General Historie of Plantes* (London, 1597), p. 72.

21 H. Thomas et al., 'Evolution, Physiology and Phytochemistry of the Psychotoxic Arable Mimic Weed Darnel (*Lolium temulentum* L.)', *Progress in Botany*, 72 (2011), pp. 73–104.

Further Reading

Abbott, E., *Sugar: A Bittersweet History* (London, 2010)

Arber, A., *The Gramineae: A Study of Cereal, Bamboo, and Grass* (Cambridge, 1934)

Bell, A. D., and A. Bryan, *Plant Form: An Illustrated Guide to Flowering Plant Morphology* (Portland, OR, 2008)

Burroughs, W. J., *Climate Change in Prehistory: The End of the Reign of Chaos* (Cambridge, 2005)

Chang, T. T., 'Rice – *Oryza sativa* and *Oryza glaberrima* (Gramineae-Oryzeae)', in *Evolution of Crop Plants*, ed. J. Smartt and N. W. Simmonds (London, 1995), pp. 147–55

Cochran, G., and H. Harpending, *The 10,000 Year Explosion: How Civilization Accelerated Human Evolution* (New York, 2009)

Crosby, A. W., *Ecological Imperialism: The Biological Expansion of Europe, 900–1900* (Cambridge, 1986)

—, *The Columbian Exchange: Biological and Cultural Consequences of 1492* (Westport, CT, 2003)

Dunmire, W. M., *Gardens of New Spain: How Mediterranean Plants and Foods Changed America* (Austin, TX, 2004)

Evans, L. T., *Feeding the Ten Billion: Plants and Population Growth* (Cambridge, 1998)

Gibson, D. J., *Grasses and Grassland Ecology* (Oxford, 2009)

Glémin, S., and T. Bataillon, 'A Comparative View of the Evolution of Grasses under Domestication', *New Phytologist*, 183 (2009), pp. 273–90

Godfray, H.C.J., et al., 'Food Security: the Challenge of Feeding 9 Billion People', *Science*, 327 (2010), pp. 812–18

Harlan, J. R., *Crops and Man* (Madison, WI, 1992)

Harvey, G., *The Forgiveness of Nature: The Story of Grass* (London, 2002)

Hibberd, J. M., et al., 'Using C_4 Photosynthesis to Increase the Yield of Rice – Rationale and Feasibility', *Current Opinion in Plant Biology*, 11 (2008), pp. 228–31

Hudson, N. W., *Soil Conservation* (London, 1981)

Jacobs, B. F., et al., 'The Origin of Grass-dominated Ecosystems', *Annals of the Missouri Botanical Garden*, 86 (1999), pp. 590–643

Jain, H. K., *The Green Revolution: History, Impact and Future* (Houston, TX, 2010)

Jenkins, V. S., *The Lawn: A History of an American Obsession* (Washington, DC, 1994)

Juma, C., *The Gene Hunters: Biotechnology and the Scramble for Seeds* (Princeton, NJ, 1989)

Kellogg, E. A., 'Evolutionary History of the Grasses', *Plant Physiology*, 125 (2001), pp. 1198–205

Kingsbury, N., *Hybrid: The History and Science of Plant Breeding* (Chicago, IL, 2009)

Mann, C. C., *1493: How Europe's Discovery of the Americas Revolutionized Trade, Ecology and Life on Earth* (London, 2011)

Mazoyer, M., and L. Roudart, *A History of World Agriculture from the Neolithic Age to the Current Crisis* (London, 2006)

Morton, A. G., *History of Botanical Science: an Account of the Development of Botany from Ancient Times to the Present Day* (London, 1981)

Murphy, D. J., *People, Plants and Genes: The Story of Crops and Humanity* (Oxford, 2007)

Nabhan, G. P., *Where Our Food Comes From: Retracing Nikolay Vavilov's Quest to End Famine* (Washington, DC, 2008)

Ó Gráda, C., *Famine: A Short History* (Princeton, NJ, 2009)

Phillips, S. T., 'Lessons from the Dust Bowl: Dryland Agriculture and Soil Erosion in the United States and South Africa, 1900–1950', *Environmental History*, 4 (1999), pp. 245–66

Purseglove, J. W., *Tropical Crops: Monocotyledons 1* (London, 1972)

Roach, B. T., 'Sugar Canes', in *Evolution of Crop Plants*, ed. J. Smartt and N. W. Simmonds (London, 1995), pp. 160–6

Royal Society, *Reaping the Benefits: Science and the Sustainable Intensification of Global Agriculture*. RS Policy document 11/09 (London, 2009)

Ruddiman, W. F., *Plows, Plagues, and Petroleum: How Humans Took Control of Climate* (Princeton, NJ, 2005)

Sage, R. F., 'The Evolution of C_4 Photosynthesis', *New Phytologist*, 161 (2004), pp. 341–70

Smith, B. D., *The Emergence of Agriculture* (New York, 1998)

Solomon et al., S., *Contribution of Working Group 1 to the Fourth Assessment Report of the Intergovernmental Panel on Climate Change, 2007* (Cambridge, 2007)

Staller, J., *Maize Cobs and Cultures: History of Zea mays L:* (Berlin, 2010)

Thomson, P., *Seeds, Sex and Civilization* (London, 2010)

Werger, M.J.A., and M. A. van Staalduinen, *Eurasian Steppes: Ecological Problems and Livelihoods in a Changing World* (Berlin, 2012)

Wright, H. A., and A. W. Bailey, *Fire Ecology: United States and Southern Canada* (New York, 1982)

Zohary, D., and M. Hopf, *Domestication of Plants in the Old World* (Oxford, 2000)

Associations and Websites

GRASSBASE
The online world grass flora
www.kew.org/data/grasses-db

ANGIOSPERM PHYLOGENY WEBSITE
www.mobot.org/MOBOT/research/APweb

FOOD AND AGRICULTURE ORGANIZATION OF THE UNITED NATIONS
www.fao.org

CIMMYT
International Maize and Wheat Improvement Center
www.cimmyt.org

IRRI
International Rice Research Institute
http://irri.org

INBAR
International Network for Bamboo and Rattan
www.inbar.int

Associations

EUCARPIA
European Association for Research on Plant Breeding
www.eucarpia.org

AMERICAN BAMBOO SOCIETY
www.bamboo.org

BRITISH GRASSLAND SOCIETY
www.britishgrassland.com

CALIFORNIA NATIVE GRASSLANDS ASSOCIATION
http://cnga.org

TURFGRASS GROWERS ASSOCIATION
www.turfgrass.co.uk

UNICA
Brazilian Sugarcane Industry Association
http://english.unica.com.br

BAMBOO GARDEN
www.bamboogarden.com

LA BAMBOUSERAIE DE PRAFRANCE
www.bambouseraie.fr

Acknowledgements

I would like to thank Professor Liam Dolan for his enthusiasm for this book and Dr Caroline Pannell for reading and commenting on the manuscript.

Photo Acknowledgements

❦

The author and the publishers wish to express their thanks to the below sources of illustrative material and /or permission to reproduce it.

Agricultural Research Service, USDA: pp. 59 (Michael Thompson), 76, 97 (Keith Weller), 84 (Doug Wilson), 100 (David Nance), 125 (Jack Dykinga), 134 (Scott Bauer); © The Trustees of the British Museum, London: pp. 20, 32, 54, 55, 62, 66, 69, 81, 83, 92, 96, 109, 112, 130, 132, 133; S. A. Harris: pp. 10, 11, 13, 23, 29, 31, 37, 41, 43, 44−5, 48, 51, 53, 90, 104−5, 117, 128, 145, 150, 153, 156, 157, 162−3, 165, 180, 181, 184; Michael Leaman: p. 39; Metropolitan Museum of Art, New York: pp. 28, 65; Oxford University Herbaria: pp. 6, 34, 78, 94, 120, 137, 176; personal collections: pp. 12, 16, 19, 21, 23, 73, 75, 107, 115, 144, 159, 171, 183, 184; Yale Center for British Art, New Haven: pp. 116, 146, 147, 164, 168−9, 170.

Index